In a world filled with people [...]
great, Christians should aim t[...]
Kendall's book *For an Audien[...]
world filled with people living [...] popularity on social
media today, Christians should concern themselves with God's
glory for all eternity. If your soul is weary of this foolish and
fallen world, it's time to start living for an audience of One.
This is the one thing that changes everything.

—Mark Driscoll
Founding and Senior Pastor, The Trinity Church
Author, *Win Your War*, *Spirit-Filled Jesus*,
and *Real Marriage*

Not too long before my daddy died, he called me to his bedside
and said, "You must always remember to stay focused."

"On what, Daddy?" I asked.

"On the cross and the person of Jesus Christ," he responded.

I have had the privilege of knowing R. T. Kendall for
several years. When he told me the title of his newest book,
I thought that R. T. knows what he is talking about because,
like my daddy, his desire is to always focus on the cross and
the person of Jesus Christ. And this is what living a life for an
audience of One is all about.

—Gigi Graham

I cannot imagine a timelier book than R. T. Kendall's *For an
Audience of One.* In it he points us to the true purpose of
every believer: we are to lay down every aspect of our lives,
giving God all of the glory. The dying time is essential for
every believer, but the duration is up to us. It took Israel forty
years; it took Jesus forty days. These pages are filled with true
humility. They hold the priceless wisdom of a man who has

walked faithfully with God over a lifetime. As you read this book, let R. T.'s words challenge and focus you. We cannot discover our significance on the earth until we've truly come face to face with our insignificance. Everything good in us is by His grace. I absolutely love this book!

—BILL JOHNSON
BETHEL CHURCH, REDDING, CALIFORNIA
AUTHOR, *THE WAY OF LIFE* AND *RAISING GIANT-KILLERS*

For an
AUDIENCE
of

One

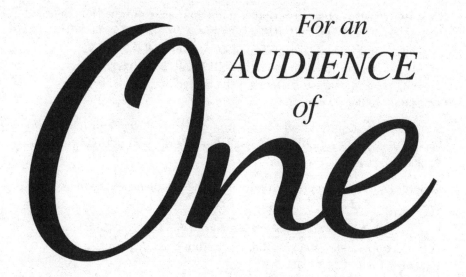

For an
AUDIENCE
of
One

R. T. KENDALL

CHARISMA
HOUSE

For an Audience of One by R. T. Kendall
Published by Charisma House
Charisma Media/Charisma House Book Group
600 Rinehart Road, Lake Mary, Florida 32746

Visit the author's website at www.rtkendallministries.com.
Library of Congress Cataloging-in-Publication Data

Names: Kendall, R. T., 1935- author.
Title: For an audience of one / by R. T. Kendall.
Description: Lake Mary, Florida : Charisma House, [2020] | Includes bibliographical references.
Identifiers: LCCN 2019037321 (print) | LCCN 2019037322 (ebook) | ISBN 9781629996738 (trade paperback) | ISBN 9781629996745 (ebook)
Subjects: LCSH: Christian life--Biblical teaching. | Judgment of God. | God (Christianity)--Worship and love.
Classification: LCC BS680.C47 K46 2020 (print) | LCC BS680.C47 (ebook) |

DDC 248.4--dc23

LC record available at https://lccn.loc.gov/2019037321

LC ebook record available at https://lccn.loc.gov/2019037322

20 21 22 23 24 — 9 8 7 6 5 4 3 2 1

Printed in the United States of America

Let us thus think often that our only business in this life is to please God, that perhaps all besides is but folly and vanity.

—Nicolas Herman,
known as Brother Lawrence (1614–1691),
The Practice of the Presence of God

To Toby, Timothy, and Ty

CONTENTS

FOREWORD

NEXT TO THE apostle Paul, no evangelist has impacted the world for Jesus Christ more than the late Billy Graham. Included among the millions who came to Christ under his preaching was my own mother. For fifty-four years Dr. Graham was a member of First Baptist Church, Dallas, where I pastor, and he made an indelible mark on my life and ministry.

I am delighted that my friend Dr. R. T. Kendall has chosen Dr. Graham as one of the examples in his latest book. I have read a number of R. T.'s books over the years. His book on the life of Joseph, *God Meant It for Good*, is one of his most popular and was a blessing to me years ago. The present book, *For An Audience of One*, will almost certainly stand alongside his book on Joseph. It is R. T.'s unfolding of what he calls his "life verse"—John 5:44: "How can ye believe, which receive honour one of another, and seek not the honour that cometh from God only?" (KJV). A quick way to grasp the point of this book, as he himself puts it, is this: Billy Graham preached to millions but in fact preached for an audience of One. R. T.'s hope is that the reader will be persuaded to resist the praise of man and live as though only God was looking on. If we could live like this, truly our lives would be changed forever.

Born in Ashland, Kentucky, nearly eighty-five years ago, R. T. was a Southern Baptist pastor before attending Southern Baptist Theological Seminary in Louisville, Kentucky. He received an MDiv from Southern Baptist Seminary and went on to receive a DPhil in theology from Oxford University. His thesis, entitled *Calvin and English Calvinism to 1648*, was published by Oxford University Press. He was called to be the senior minister of Westminster Chapel in 1977, following men such as Dr. G. Campbell Morgan and Dr. Martyn Lloyd-Jones. Retiring from Westminster Chapel after twenty-five years, he has had an itinerant ministry all over the world and continues to write books.

It is my prayer that his latest book that honors Dr. Graham will be a motivation for you, as it has been for me, to live "for an audience of One."

—DR. ROBERT JEFFRESS
PASTOR, FIRST BAPTIST CHURCH, DALLAS

SPECIAL RECOMMENDATION

I HAVE WORKED IN the harsh competitive world of finance for over forty years, and one thing I know for certain is that James Bond gets it right when he says, "The world is not enough."[1] There is a longing and thirst for purpose and fulfillment in life that the world cannot give. We are a generation looking for likes yet longing for love. As we desperately search for fulfillment and seek to find the secret to human flourishing, we frequently go to the wrong places and people to find it. As I have mentored many young millennial leaders over the years, the thread woven throughout the fabric of all our conversations is the pressure to prove oneself and to get others to affirm and validate one's worth. In doing so, we forget that we were created to live for an audience of One, the One who created, forgave, and redeemed us.

As I ponder this cultural landscape that presents itself

before us, I can think of no better or more urgent book to hold in your hands than this new book by my good friend Dr. R. T. Kendall titled *For An Audience of One.*

R. T. reminds us that there is no higher approval that a person can enjoy and rest in than to know he or she has pleased God, and such treasure lasts for eternity.

This book is the distillation of R. T.'s deep biblical knowledge and depth of understanding gained from his many years as a theologian, writer, and pastor and as an astute observer of Christians struggling in this area. I found his book incredibly insightful, specifically in three areas.

First this book is informative. With biblical precision and practical advice R. T. addresses the global epidemic of living for people's applause and approval and encourages us to focus on living for the audience of One. R. T. spends time deconstructing the world's priorities for approval and rebuilds our faith by exegeting the biblical texts that are case studies for us, showing how prominent people pleasing has been throughout the generations and informing us that we too are not immune to such vices—particularly as we are tempted toward pride and can often be desensitized to hearing the voice and commands of God.

Second I found this book reminded me of the need for greater intentionality when fighting the need to please. R. T. paints a hopeful picture of the strength a believer can have by following Jesus' example. Jesus was resolute and determined in living out His core story, to die for the sins of humanity. He wasn't intimidated by the religious leaders. He wasn't insecure because of their opposition; instead He intentionally moved toward Calvary, knowing that was what He came to do. In a world that is fighting for our attention, we must be intentional in asking, What does God want for my life? And what does He want me to do, as opposed to everybody else's expectations? R.T. has spent his life prioritizing the pursuit of seeking the approval of God alone and resisting the temptation to conform or submit to the status quo. His favorite Bible verse addresses such a stronghold: "How can you believe since you accept glory from one another but do not seek the glory that comes from the only God?" (John 5:44).

Finally I found this book instructive. It is a much-needed resource that is grounded in practical application that will enable you to apply in your everyday life the biblical principles R.T. paints for us. R.T. exposes the idols that cause us to lean toward people's approval, and by exposing them, he reminds us that the devil loses his edge. I am often reminded of these idols that threaten to steal my focus from pleasing God alone, and when that happens, it's like drinking from wells of water that never truly satisfy: "broken cisterns that cannot hold water" (Jer. 2:13).

I have no doubt that as you turn the pages of this book, the words of R.T. will resonate with your spirit and remind you that the affirmation of others makes a wonderful supplement to the approval of God, but a terrible substitute. I am challenged and encouraged once again to continue to walk out my Christian faith for the audience of One and live for the applause of nail-scarred hands.

—KEN COSTA
AUTHOR, FRIEND, FINANCIER

PREFACE

I HAVE BEEN BLESSED with surprising open doors in my old age—both with writing and speaking. I pray daily to know when to say yes and when I must say no. I find it hard to say no. I also pray earnestly to know what book I should write next. I still have books in me, not to mention hundreds of unpublished sermons and Bible studies I delivered at Westminster Chapel during my twenty-five years there.

When I heard a sermon by Bruce Atkinson, a previous associate pastor of London's Kensington Temple, titled, "An Audience of One," I told him immediately I wanted that to be the title of my next book—based upon my life verse. A few days later I read a tribute to Billy Graham (1918–2018) by Sam Hailes, editor of UK's *Premier Christianity*, who stated that Billy's secret was that, although he preached to millions, he "lived for an audience of One." I have since discovered that Bill Johnson at Bethel Church in Redding, California, has spoken on the subject "living before an audience of One." That sums up what this book is about. The "One" throughout this book of course refers to the Trinitarian God—Father, Son, and Holy Spirit.

This book is dedicated to our three grandsons: Tobias Robert, Timothy Robert, and Tyndale Robert. I was not prepared for how much they would mean to Louise and me or how much I would love them. I pray for them daily that they will be like the three Hebrew children—Shadrach, Meshach, and Abednego—who chose the burning fiery furnace over bowing down to Nebuchadnezzar's golden image (Dan. 3). When all of them are old enough to read this book, it is my heart's cry that the Holy Spirit will grip them to choose to live their lives before an audience of One.

INTRODUCTION

I NEVER WILL FORGET a story I heard years ago. A young prodigy—a pianist—gave his first concert at the Royal Festival Hall in London. His reputation preceded him; the concert was sold out on the day that tickets were first available. His brilliance at the piano exceeded all expectancy. When he finished his last piece, the audience went wild. They stood to their feet spontaneously and shouted and cheered.

The young pianist bowed quickly and hurried off stage. But the audience was begging for him to come back. The stage manager whispered to him, "Go quickly—they are yelling for you."

But the young man wasn't moving. Instead he peered through a crack in the curtain, anxiously scanning the audience.

"No, I can't go out there," he said.

The stage manager was bordering on annoyance: "Look, son, they are on their feet. Trust me; they don't do this for everybody—go out and enjoy it."

The boy continued to scan the audience.

Finally the stage manager cracked; he shouted, "Get out there—they are standing for you!"

The young pianist looked at him and whispered, "They are not all standing. Do you see the old man in the last row from the back? He is still seated."

"Who cares about one old man?" said the stage manager.

The boy answered with a steely determination. "I care. That's my teacher. When he stands, I can take that bow."

The crowds were still cheering, two thousand people applauding his skill, his brilliance, the sheer magic of his music. But the young musician knew in his heart that none of that mattered unless his teacher—his mentor—approved.

In truth he was playing for an audience of…one.

The humility of this young prodigy is in contrast to a scene at London's Heathrow Airport. There was a man in a hurry, but he was tenth in line at Heathrow. For some reason there was no agent working at the business class desk. This man was used to special treatment, used to being in the priority line. He also took himself very seriously. He seethed that he had to wait his turn. He suddenly broke all the rules of etiquette and fair play: he jumped to the front of the line. He said to the check-in person: "Madam, *do you know who I am*?" The shrewd lady immediately picked up a phone and made an announcement that came over the loudspeakers: "There's a man at desk fourteen who does not know his name. So if you know who this might be, would you please come and help him?"

As it happens, that man was not me, but I'm afraid it could have been. I have done the equivalent of that more times than I want to admit. If I could only remember that God in heaven is watching my every move and listening to every word! As the old spiritual put it:

He sees all you do, He hears all you say; my Lord is writing all the time.

—ANONYMOUS

Malachi speaks of a scroll of remembrance:

Then those who feared the LORD talked with each other, and the LORD listened and heard. A scroll of remembrance was written in his presence concerning those who feared the LORD and honored his name

—MALACHI 3:16

Think of these words: *the Lord listened and heard.*

If you and I could keep this in mind, that the Lord God of heaven and earth—Father, Son, and Holy Spirit—is listening to each word we say, I think it would change our lives. My most unfavorite verse in the Bible is this—the very words of Jesus:

I tell you that everyone will have to give account on the day of judgment for every empty word they have spoken.

—MATTHEW 12:36

To put it another way: if we could intentionally imagine an audience of One—Jesus Himself—is eavesdropping on our every conversation, it could save us from a lot of regret and stress. An unguarded comment, which James calls a "spark," can set a forest on fire (Jas. 3:5).

James went on to say that there are two kinds of wisdom: 1) wisdom from heaven—true wisdom and 2) "wisdom"— namely counterfeit wisdom, which is from the devil. The difference is that wisdom that comes from heaven is "first of all pure; then peace-loving, considerate, submissive, full of mercy and good fruit, impartial and sincere." The "wisdom" that comes from below invariably results in envy, selfish ambition, disorder and "every evil practice" (vv. 15–17).

Heavenly but practical wisdom is what the Book of Proverbs is mainly about. It has nothing to do with your education, intelligence, or being well connected. It begins with the fear of the Lord (Prov. 1:7; 9:10). Its importance can hardly be exaggerated:

> The beginning of wisdom is this: Get wisdom. Though it cost all you have, get understanding. Cherish her, and she will exalt you; embrace her, and she will honor you. She will give you a garland to grace your head and present you with a glorious crown.
>
> —PROVERBS 4:7–9

THE PURPOSE OF THIS BOOK

The purpose of this book is fourfold:

1. to lead you to experience the conscious approval of God;

2. to lead you to experience the joy of knowing you live to serve the Creator of the world;

3. to lead you to have godly wisdom; and

4. to show the way forward that will save you from regret down the road.

In truth all those fourfold aims can be summed up very simply: it is so that on that final day you will not only not be ashamed but full of joy as you come face to face with...an audience of One.

Being motivated and governed by making the Lord Jesus Christ your audience of One will lead you to these four things. I guarantee it.

That said, there is one predominant, consistent truth that is an assumption on every page of this book: the God of the Bible is a jealous God. He is unashamedly and unapologetically *jealous.* That is who He is. This turns some people off; it turns some people on. It turns me on. I love it. It means He loves me and cares for me and ensures that no good thing will be withheld from me if I love His glory (Ps. 84:11).

What I want to convey in this book is that if we could *remember* to speak and act as though there were no one else present but Jesus Christ Himself, it could be life-changing.

The truth is, whether we remember this or not, God *is* watching and listening. And remembering. The day of judgment is what Paul calls the judgment seat of Christ: "We must all appear before the judgment seat of Christ, so that each of us may receive what is due us for the things done while in the body, whether good or bad" (2 Cor. 5:10).

That will be the scariest day of your life and mine. There is no way to calculate how dreadful and full of anxiety we will feel when that day comes. But, like it or not, it's coming. Soon.

Walk with me now. I'd love it if you would consider that you and I are on a journey together. We may be aware of each other of course. But to the degree we are conscious that He is looking at us over our shoulders and listening to every single word...to that degree will we be given pause. To stop. Wait. Think. Just maybe it will help us to be "quick to listen, slow to speak and slow to become angry" (Jas. 1:19).

Chapter One

WHAT'S IN IT FOR GOD?

———⊰•⊱———

Where, then, is boasting? It is excluded.
—ROMANS 3:27

The only evidence that I have seen the Divine Glory
is my willingness to forsake any claim upon God.
—N. BURNETT MAGRUDER (1915–2005)

W"HAT DO YOU want most in all the world?" That was a question put to me by Sergei Nikolaev, my Russian translator, also a pastor, when I was visiting the Soviet Union in 1985. I immediately replied: "To see revival in Westminster Chapel."

"Why do you want to see revival in Westminster Chapel?" he asked. I was really annoyed that he asked this. What an impertinent question! After all, why wouldn't I want to see revival in my church? Wouldn't any pastor want this?

But Sergei wouldn't back down. He pushed me: "*Why* do you want this?" To my embarrassment I struggled to answer him. Not that he said it, but I could feel his thinking...that revival in my church would be more of an ego trip for me than I wanted to admit. I did not want to face what was a part of my true motive. I rationalized by thoughts and explained to him how wonderful it would surely be if true revival came to a London church. Whereas he probably thought Moscow was the center of the world, it is surely London!

I have thought a lot about his question and that conversation. It took me longer than I care to admit to see that my motive was not as pure, impeccable, and God glorifying as I thought. However, that conversation helped shape the wording of a prayer covenant I introduced to the members of Westminster Chapel several years later in 1994. We designed a prayer covenant to be prayed daily (three hundred people signed up) that included this petition: "We pray for the manifestation of God's glory in our midst along with an ever-increasing openness in us to the manner in which God chooses to manifest that glory."

There are two things to be noted by the wording of this petition:

1. Instead of praying for revival we asked for the manifestation of God's glory.

2. We knew from church history that God can manifest Himself in strange ways; I wanted our sophisticated Brits to be open to *any* way God may choose to show up.

Did God answer our prayer? Yes. Does that mean true revival came to Westminster Chapel? No. God manifested His glory mainly by passing us by! Oh yes. That is God's right to do! What is more, He went elsewhere, as I will show later. After all, whose glory was at stake? Mine or His? Ours or His?

For sixty years I have preached the sovereignty of God. The heart of this teaching is summed up in God's word to Moses, "I will have mercy on whom I will have mercy, and I will have compassion on whom I will have compassion" (Exod. 33:19; Rom.9:15). It is one thing to believe this theoretically—especially when it comes to God's prerogative to save whom He will—but to apply the same principle to ourselves when we so desperately wanted to see revival in Westminster means we had to practice what we preached!

When we pursue the glory of God, we must remember we are pursuing whatever glorifies, honors, and pleases *Him*. This means we must personally bow out entirely and respect what *He* is pleased to do. Whenever He is pleased to do it. Wherever He is pleased to do it. With whomever He is pleased to use. We need to be willing to affirm His right to pass us by and bless those He chooses to bless—even when that blessing does not include what we hoped for.

It is one thing to preach this, another to practice it.

In a word, I think my desire for revival was more personal

than I was willing to admit. My desire was not as honoring to God as I had convinced myself to believe. I think Sergei could see this when I couldn't.

Yes, it hurt a bit when God chose to show up in power at London's Holy Trinity Brompton in 1994. I was so sure that if revival came to the world, it would come to England. If revival came to England, it would come to London. And if it came to London, it would come to Westminster Chapel—the bastion of Reformed theology. Reformed theology is all about God and His honor and glory. Not only that, but we put ourselves on the line by going to the streets of Victoria and Westminster, handing out tracts and presenting the gospel to whomever would stand still for a few moments. We believed in the Great Commission, to go into all the world to preach the gospel to all creation (Mark 16:15), as much as we believed in the sovereignty of God. We equally believed in the manifestation of the Spirit as much as we did upholding the Word. In fact I got into deep trouble with some of my members by doing things such as witnessing in the streets as well as making other changes. Surely God would honor this!

As if this obligated God to us! Or that we were entitled to His blessing! I'm afraid it wasn't *entirely* His glory after all that I had in mind; I wanted my dad, my friends, and my enemies to see Westminster Chapel right in the middle of a great move of God.

Jeremiah, a godly prophet, said that the heart is deceitful above all things and incurably wicked (Jer. 17:9). Once you think you have a handle on your heart and motives as well as your ego, lo and behold, you find out you have not arrived after all. For example, I might have thought that since we at Westminster Chapel were praying for the manifestation of the "glory of God," God would surely honor precisely that; after all He is a God of glory! In other words, I might have thought I had some sort of a claim upon God that guaranteed that God would certainly honor such a noble petition! Wrong.

I have lived long enough to observe how God blesses people of all kinds of theological streams. For example, Reformed theology may be God honoring, but God is not obligated to honor *it*—or those who uphold it!

ANOTHER CONVERSATION

This takes me back to a pivotal conversation I had in 1956. I was seated in a church service next to Dr. N. Burnett Magruder, one of my early mentors. I said to him, "Dr. Magruder, I reckon that the highest level of devotion to God would be to die as a martyr for the gospel." I wanted to see if he would agree. He smiled. He took out a sheet of paper, wrote on it and handed it to me. I was sobered. I carried his handwritten note with me for years besides writing it in my Bible. It said:

> The only evidence that I have seen the Divine Glory is my willingness to forsake any claim upon God.

Dr. Magruder was a graduate of Yale Divinity School where he studied, grasped, and was shaped by the theology of Jonathan Edwards (1703–1758)—also a graduate of Yale. Edwards is still widely regarded as America's greatest theologian but is perhaps best known for his memorable sermon "Sinners in the Hands of an Angry God," preached on July 8, 1741, in Enfield, Connecticut, at the height of the Great Awakening. What Dr. Magruder wrote on that sheet of paper reflects the thinking of Jonathan Edwards.

"Seeing" the divine glory is something John the Apostle referred to near the beginning of the fourth Gospel. "We have seen his glory, the glory of the one and only Son, who came from the Father, full of grace and truth" (John 1:14). Seeing the glory of God in Christ was to affirm Him for being just like He is. In other words, loving God for who He is in Himself apart from what He might do for us.

I anticipate that some readers may need time to absorb this. I know I did. I have tried to plumb the depths of this principle for over sixty years. I am still not able to unpack this in a sentence or two. But here is a brief introduction to what it means:

1. As long as I believe that God owes me something, I have not truly affirmed His glory; I am still thinking of what He might do for me.

2. As long as I feel entitled to something from Him, I have not truly seen His glory; I am thinking of myself.

3. As long as I think I have a *claim* on Him so that He is obligated to answer my prayers and do things for me, I have not yet seen His glory; I am still thinking of myself.

4. But when I truly see His glory, I will release Him to do what He pleases to do—whether or not I am the recipient of His blessing.

5. I will honor what He does or does not do. Whatever He does. Wherever He does it. Whenever He does it. With whomever He chooses to use—even if He bypasses me.

There is a story that lies behind one of the great hymns written by the blind composer Fanny Crosby (1820–1915). She was addressing a group of people in a prison on a Sunday afternoon. She quoted Romans 9:15, "I will have mercy on whom I will have mercy, and I will have compassion on whom I will have compassion." She was making the point that God is not obligated to save anyone but could pass us by and be just. Apparently the power of the Lord was present. A prisoner cried out, "O Lord, don't pass by me." Crosby went home and wrote a hymn that begins with these words:

> Pass me not, O gentle Savior,
> Hear my humble cry;
> While on others Thou art calling,
> Do not pass me by.[1]

In John chapter 6 you have the hard sayings of Jesus. At the beginning of the chapter Jesus had a great following—five thousand people. He fed them with five barley loaves and two small fish. But Jesus saw what their motives really were. They came, and He said to them, "You are looking for me, not because you saw the signs I performed but because you ate the loaves and had your fill" (v. 26). Everything Jesus said to them after that was offensive to them. The straw that broke the camel's back was His closing comment: "No one can come to me unless the Father who sent me draws them....*From this time* many of his disciples turned back and no longer followed him" (vv. 44, 66, emphasis added).

You could make a case that the five thousand surely saw the glory of God when they saw the *miracles*. But according to Jesus, that was not what enthralled them; it was the food. It was a "What's in it for me?" kind of following. When the thousands turned away, Jesus asked the Twelve, "You do not want to leave too, do you?" Simon Peter spoke up: "Lord, to whom shall we go? You have the words of eternal life. We have come to believe and to know that you are the Holy One of God" (vv. 67–69). In other words, unlike the five thousand, Peter worshipped Jesus for *what he saw in Jesus*—that He was the Holy One of God. This is what John meant by "seeing" Christ's glory (John 1:14).

We truly see the glory of God when we worship Him *not* for what He can do for us but for His being just like He is.

In a word: we have begun to see the glory of God when we voluntarily put ourselves out of the picture. I must not want Him to have 50 percent of the glory and me 50 percent. I must not want Him to have 90 percent of the glory and me 10 percent. I don't even want Him to have 99 percent of the glory and me 1 percent. I want Him to have *all* the glory—100 percent.

> Not to us, LORD, not to us but to your name be the glory.... Our God is in the heavens; he does whatever pleases him.
>
> —PSALM 115:1, 3

Therefore until I *see this for myself* and *love it*, I have not really *seen* His glory. Jonathan Edwards taught that one thing Satan cannot produce in us is a *love for God's glory*. If therefore you and I love God's glory, really and truly love it, we may be sure that God has performed a work of true grace in us. For Satan would not, or could not, do that. The flesh cannot do that. Only God can do this.

The flesh hates the God of glory. To quote Edwards, "Men naturally are God's enemy."[2] So if a person struggles to love a God of glory, he or she is confirming our point; there is nothing

9

about this kind of God that we naturally like. Some people are at home with a God they can either control or who is certainly equal with them. This makes God a partner—on equal footing with us. There are people who love that kind of God. But to love the God of the Bible—a God who is all-knowing, sovereign, and omnipotent—is something that comes by the Holy Spirit changing us internally. This is why Jesus said that no one could come to Him unless the Father draws him (John 6:44); it is what the Spirit does.

Most theology taught today is anthropology; it is man-centered. You and I are living in the "me generation." People only ask, "What's in it for me?" No one seems to ask, "What's in it for God?"

I would gladly spend the rest of my life getting people to ask the question, "What's in it for God?"

For example, what was in it for God when Jesus died on the cross? The answer: it is what satisfied His justice; the blood of Jesus turned His wrath away. There is a big word that describes this; it is called propitiation. Paul said that God presented Jesus "as a propitiation by His blood" (Rom. 3:25, NKJV). John said that Jesus is "the propitiation for our sins, and not for ours only but also for the sins of the whole world" (1 John 2:2, NKJV). It comes from the Greek word *hilasterion*. It refers to the lid of the ark of the covenant. It is translated "mercy seat" in Hebrews 9:5. On the ancient day of atonement the blood sprinkled on the mercy seat is when and where the atonement took effect.

God's plan of salvation has been designed in such a manner that "no one may boast before him" (1 Cor. 1:29). Paul said that we are justified by faith—faith plus nothing. Works are completely and totally out of the picture, says Paul, insofar as contributing to our salvation. He then posed a question, "Where, then, is boasting?" He answers: "It is excluded" (Rom. 3:27). Had Abraham been justified by works, he had something to boast about—"but not before God" (Rom. 4:2).

If you ask, "Where do works come in?" the answer is:

1. They show our gratitude to God for such a free salvation (Rom. 12).

2. They demonstrate to the world that we care for their needs (Jas. 2).

The bottom line: God gets all the glory. We cannot boast that we did anything to bring about our salvation. He did it all—from start to finish; He enabled us to come to Christ and believe. It is faith alone in Christ alone.

The Bible is a God-centered book. The Holy Spirit wrote it (2 Tim. 3:15; 2 Pet. 1:21). It is designed to give God all the glory. "I will not yield my glory to another," He says (Isa. 42:8). This is why the doctrine of salvation removes any person from boasting if they are saved.

What I have described in this chapter is a bare glimpse of the nature of the true God—the One who watches over us day and night and who listens to all we say. What a privilege it is for us to have a heavenly Father like that! What is more, He only wants what is best for us. No good thing will He withhold from us when we do what we do and say what we say for an audience of One.

Chapter Two

KNOWING THAT GOD KNOWS

I do not know—God knows.
—2 CORINTHIANS 12:2

For one who is not prescient of all future things is not God.
—ST. AUGUSTINE (354–430)

C AN YOUR WIFE be your enemy?" That question came from a minister in Northern Ireland after I preached a sermon on praying for your enemies. "Yes," I replied. That conversation led me to insert a chapter called "An Unhappy Marriage" in my book *Thorn in the Flesh*. Paul coined the phrase "thorn in the flesh" to describe an extreme form of God's chastening, or disciplining. Paul said that God sent it to him to keep him humble—to keep him from being conceited or admired too much (2 Cor. 12:7).

Paul admitted to needing a thorn in the flesh. If he needed it, how much more do I need it! Do you need a thorn in the flesh? Paul stated that he needed this because he had seen so many revelations and visions. These experiences of God could tempt him to boast a lot. So in order to keep him from being exalted too much, God sent this thorn in the flesh to him—a painful nuisance that would not go away although he asked God three times to remove it.

In introducing his thorn in the flesh, the apostle Paul refers to one of his visions—when he was translated to the "third heaven." Whether this experience was "in the body or out of the body I do not know—God knows," says Paul (2 Cor. 12:2).

"God knows"—possibly a throwaway comment—forms the foundation for this book and especially this chapter.

Speaking personally, the very knowledge that *God knows* is what has served to motivate me to live for an audience of One. I would hope that knowing God knows should motivate you also to live and speak before an audience of One. He is fully aware of what is going on, what I am thinking, and what I say. The God of glory is my audience of One. When I write, I am, of course, aware of you my reader, but I am mainly writing for Him. It is His approval, not yours, I am after. When I preach,

I am speaking before God although I am aware of my listeners. When I speak to my wife, I am conscious of what I say, but I must keep in mind that He is listening. When I speak to people—whether to thousands or to one person on a plane, on a train, at a ticket counter, or on the telephone—I must remember that God knows what I am saying. He knows *why* I am saying it. He knows my true motive. If I did not believe that God knows what I am thinking at every moment, I would not need to watch what I say or do. The truth is, whether I like it or not, He does know. It is what motivates me to be a better person in all I think, say, and do.

However, as we will see further later, the knowledge that He knows is the most comforting thought I can think of. He knows when I am low. When I am mistreated. When I am spoken evil of. When I am lied about. When I am under financial pressure. When I am ill. When I am depressed. God knows. Hallelujah!

And yet what is most sobering, often painful, is that God knows my *true* motive in what I do! I can play games with myself, but when I pause and reflect that He knows exactly *why* I am up to something, it often stops me from making a foolish mistake.

If you are like me, one of the most common faults we make is to run ahead of the Lord. Joseph and Mary did this. They went a whole day's journey, "thinking he was in their company" (Luke 2:44), but He wasn't. It is so easy to assume the Lord approves of our plans merely because we truly want to please Him, because we have spent time with Him, and have even sensed His approval in so much of what we do. And yet it is still very possible to go ahead of Him, thinking that He is behind our plans. When we move ahead like this, we are on our own. It is a precarious place to be!

THE ROAD TO JOY

A further purpose of this book is to remind you that if you constantly envision an audience of One and speak as though only Jesus Christ were listening, it will lead not only to wisdom but also to joy, not to mention saving you from so much regret down the road. But more than that, by remembering an audience of One, you honor God and give Him great pleasure. It is what pleases Him. Enoch had this testimony, that he "pleased God" (Heb. 11:5). That is what I want to do. I believe it is what you want to do, or you would probably not be reading this book.

Remembering that I speak to an audience of One twenty-four hours a day is what helps to keep me on the straight and narrow road that leads to abundant life and joy.

Joy

The fruit of the Spirit is "love, joy, peace..." (Gal. 5:22).

Dr. Martyn Lloyd-Jones preached through the Book of Romans—that is, until he came to Romans 14:17: "For the kingdom of God is not a matter of eating and drinking, but of righteousness, peace and joy in the Holy Spirit." He spent an entire sermon on righteousness and the following week on peace. It was then he went to the hospital with a condition that required surgery, which ultimately led to his retirement. After thirty years of ministry at Westminster Chapel, he never returned to the pulpit. Later he told a group of ministers that he didn't finish the sermon on verse 17 because he wasn't ready to preach on the "joy in the Holy Ghost."[1] What a vulnerable, humble statement.

We all want and need more joy. Being conscious of an audience of One is what *leads* to joy—an internal exhilaration. It is a wonderful feeling inside; an emotion evoked by knowing you please God. It comes by the inner testimony of the Holy Spirit.

Joy has sometimes been imparted by the laying on of hands, leading some people to joyous uncontrollable laughter. This phenomenon is not to be dismissed or smirked at. God graciously does this from time to time. It is very real. But that sort of joy is also temporary and needs to be augmented by a lasting joy that comes from pursuing God's glory.

A major difference between joy and happiness is that joy is internal; happiness comes from external events—financial security, material things, a compliment, or good news of any kind. You can have joy and not have happiness—that is, things around you may be horrible, but you get joy from knowing you please God.

> In heav'nly love abiding,
> No change my heart shall fear;
> And safe in such confiding,
> For nothing changes here.
> The storm may roar without me,
> My heart may low be laid,
> But God is round about me,
> And can I be dismayed?[2]
>
> —ANNA LETITIA WARING

God knows and understands what we don't know or understand.

When Paul says, "God knows," he means that only God knew whether Paul was in the body or out of the body when he was taken to the third heaven. The Greek word *know* in this passage is from *oida*. There are two important Greek words for knowledge: *gnosis* and *oida*. To oversimplify, *gnosis* tends to refer to revealed knowledge, *oida* to factual knowledge.

Therefore, when Paul says that he doesn't know whether he was in or out of the body but God knows, he means that God knows for a *fact* whether Paul was in or out of the body. God knows for sure.

GOD KNOWS EVERYTHING

Have you ever asked what God's IQ is? How intelligent is God? How much does God know? Answer: "His understanding has no limit" (Ps. 147:5). God is omniscient; He is all-wise, and He knows everything—past, present, future. A God who does not know the future is not God, said St. Augustine. According to Isaiah, God declares the end from the beginning:

> I am God, and there is no other; I am God, and there is none like me. I make known the end from the beginning, from ancient times, what is still to come. I say, "My purpose will stand, and I will do what I please."
> —ISAIAH 46:9–10

Paul actually uses *oida* two times in 2 Corinthians:

1. to show that God knows what we know (2 Cor. 11:11, 31); and

2. to show that God knows what we do not know (2 Cor. 12:2–3).

I find both truths very comforting. First, just to know that God knows. He is very aware of what we know! If you feel lonely, rejected, unwanted, marginalized, or unappreciated, remember that God *knows how you feel*. This truth has encouraged me to no end. He not only knows what we feel; Jesus our great High Priest *feels what we feel*. Although He is seated at the right hand of God, Jesus has never forgotten what it was like when He was on this earth. He is touched with the feeling of our weaknesses (Heb. 4:15). I think of the old spiritual from the nineteenth century:

> Nobody knows the troubles I've seen;
> Nobody knows but Jesus.
>
> —ANONYMOUS

The psalmist said,

> You have searched me, LORD, and you know me. You know when I sit and when I rise; you perceive my thoughts from afar. You discern my going out and my lying down; you are familiar with all my ways. Before a word is on my tongue you, LORD, know it completely.
>
> —PSALM 139:1–4

Knowing that God knows is often the simple truth that will turn us around. I've found it so a thousand times.

Second, *oida* is used by Paul to show that God knows what we do *not* know. We don't know the future, but God does. I may not know the meaning of a difficult verse in the Bible, but God knows. (I sometimes think I should write a book titled *Verses in the Bible I Don't Understand*.) I don't know why God allows evil and suffering to continue, but God knows. What is more, one day our heavenly Father—the most maligned person in the universe—will clear His name. In the meantime I often don't know the next step forward when I'm in difficulty, but God knows. That is where His infinite wisdom comes in; He knows exactly what I should do next, but if He grants me the presence of the mind of the Holy Spirit—and I follow it—I won't mess up. I love that God has an opinion on *everything* and that He is often willing to reveal His opinion if we really want it.

When it comes to prayer, God knows what we need before we tell Him or ask for something (Matt. 6:8, 32). Then why tell Him what is on our hearts if He already knows? Answer: because He wants us to! That is good enough for me. We must never become so sophisticated in our knowledge of God that we don't talk to Him as a child would. He wants us to be like children (Matt. 18:3).

Here are four things that God knows:

1. He knows our frailties. Paul calls them "weaknesses" (Heb. 4:15; "infirmities" KJV). We all have weaknesses. What may be mine may not be yours; what may be yours may not be mine. The comforting thing is my weaknesses don't cause God to be disillusioned with me. He knows all about me—my past and present— and is not put off by what He knows. He loves you and me just the same!

2. He knows our feelings. When Hagar ran from Sarai, God stepped in to show Hagar that He cared for her. She was amazed to learn that God cared: "You are the God who sees me," said Hagar (Gen. 16:13). This is why Peter could say, "Cast all your anxiety on him for he cares for you" (1 Pet. 5:7). That is the verse that came to me when I was distraught one Monday morning, October 31, 1955. The Lord allowed me to see His glory, and I was

changed forever. God knows our feelings and cares about our feelings.

3. He knows our frame. One of the most tender verses in the Bible says that God remembers that we are dust (Ps. 103:14). He knows absolutely *how* we were created—out of dust (Gen. 2:7). The psalmist actually refers to our pre-fallen state! "I praise you because I am fearfully and wonderfully made" (Ps. 139:14). We were created able to sin, said St. Augustine. God has not forgotten that. With this in mind, Augustine also said that we were not able not to sin after the fall, but able not to sin after being regenerated. But in heaven we will be unable to sin! God sees the end from the beginning and yet remembers in the meantime that we are dust!

4. He knows our future. God showed Daniel, "There is a God in heaven who reveals mysteries. He has shown King Nebuchadnezzar what will happen in days to come" (Dan. 2:28). God knows "the time of the end" (Dan. 8:17), "the distant future" (v. 26), and the exact day of Jesus' second coming (Mark 13:32). All prophecy—Old Testament and New Testament—is based upon the essential premise that God knows the future!

GOD SEES THROUGH OUR MOTIVES

But now for the most sobering and heart-searching truth of all: *God knows our true motives*. And when we remember this, we should pause and ask: "Why am I saying this?" "Why am I about to do this?"

The greatest challenge I have in writing this book is to try to explain how we can get in touch with our truest motives for what we do. Is it for money? Is it for fame? Is attraction involved? Is it to make another jealous? Is it to make others admire us?

God knows our truest motives when we are about to speak. The paramount question is this: Do *we* know our truest motives? Jeremiah 17:9 cannot be quoted too often: "The heart is deceitful above all things and beyond cure. Who can understand it?" It can be very painful indeed to see—and then to admit to—why we at times say what we say. But God instantly sees through the motives that may take days, if not years, for us to see. As Jesus knew the real motives of the five thousand: it was getting their tummies filled.

God sees our true motives at once. What is more, one day all motives will eventually be revealed: "He will bring to light what is hidden in darkness and will expose the motives of the heart" (1 Cor. 4:5). He will do it for sure at the second coming and at the judgment seat of Christ. And yet sometimes God does it before then!

I have a close friend in London, Lyndon Bowring. He is a respected Christian leader in Britain, executive chairman of Christian Action Research and Education. He knows me so well. He is one of the few people I know who will correct me, cut me down to size when I need it, but also laugh with me. I don't have to be "on duty" when I am with Lyndon. But here is my point. He knows so well how my mind works that he can stop me in mid-sentence: "Don't go there." I will say, "Let me finish." He will say, "I know where you are heading. You can't do that. You can't say that." He is almost always right.

Here is my point. An omniscient God knows me better than Lyndon does! He sees *all* my motives. But if only God would *stop* me from saying or doing something before I make a mistake. Here are ten examples of what I am talking about.

1. Accepting an invitation before I think it through.

Although I pray daily to know when to say yes and when to say no, I often say yes because it seems so sensible and convenient and the right thing to do on the surface. This could be an invitation to preach or to go out to a restaurant. I hate to say no to either, but often I lose peace merely because I feel obligated to accept someone's gracious invitation. I've heard it said that someone once asked John Stott (1921–2011) if he was free on a certain date. He looked at his diary: yes. "Oh good," said the person, "you can preach for me then." "No," said John, "I am booking that day for my private time!"

2. Making an important decision without praying sufficiently about it.

This was the mistake Joshua made when he was deceived by the Gibeonites. On the surface all seemed clear and straightforward, but they did not inquire of the Lord (Josh. 9:14). Had they done this, they would have spared themselves grief in their own generation, not to mention future generations.

Oh, what peace we often forfeit,
Oh, what needless pain we bear
All because we did not carry
Everything to God in prayer.[3]

3. Offering a word of advice before I have the right to give it.

If people ask for advice, perhaps it is fine to consider giving it; but when they don't ask, and you speak into their lives, you may be outside your right to talk to them. We all must earn the right to speak privately to people. This could be based on a longer relationship or by learning more about the person. By the way, I have learned one lesson from "prophetic" people; if you ask them for a word, so many of them will have one. My experience is that it is often worthless. Let them initiate it without your prompting. But even then that does not mean you have to accept what they say.

4. Speaking when I am annoyed.

A lesson I learned from Dr. Martyn Lloyd-Jones: "When you are agitated, don't speak." When you speak when you are annoyed, it will almost always come out wrong! I once went to see my bank manager over not getting the checks and deposit slips that had been promised. It turns out the bank manager had not kept his word. My anger showed. I had no peace until I went back and apologized. When you are agitated—even if the anger seems justified—the devil will exploit this and cause you to say what will reflect badly upon your Christian testimony. My friend Charles Carrin says that he once felt a strong impression from the Lord: "Give up your right to be angry"— even if you think you have a right to be angry!

5. Accusing another when it is really because you are holding a grudge.

You are not to judge another in the first place, says Jesus (Matt. 7:1), but when you point the finger, chances are you have a skeleton in your closet along the same line of what you are accusing them of. Jesus said, "Take the plank out of your own eye, and then you will see clearly to remove the speck from your brother's eye" (Matt. 7:5). Believe me, by the time you succeed in removing the plank from your eye—which is unlikely—the issue that made you want to judge will probably have evaporated in the meantime!

6. Saying a word that is boastful about your accomplishment for reasons of aggrandizement.

Do you need to name drop? Do you need to say something that will cause people to admire you? "Let someone else praise you, and not your own mouth" (Prov. 27:2). I have a great weakness here—as I do all these examples. But I have had a hard time resisting telling people of some famous person I met or some compliment I received. The truth is people don't really want to know about your accomplishments. This is why it is easier to weep with those who weep than rejoice with those who rejoice (Rom. 12:15). I used to ask the members of Westminster Chapel: "How many of you could have tea with Her Majesty, the Queen, and never mention it to a soul?"

7. Speaking out of fear.

Anxiety often only breeds anxiety in the other—or will irritate them. "Do not fret—it leads only to evil" (Ps. 37:8). Wait until you are calm. Remember this proverb too: "In the multitude of words sin is not lacking, but he who restrains his lips is wise" (Prov. 10:19, NKJV). It is very like the previously mentioned point—speaking when annoyed. So too with fear; when you speak out of anxiety, you likely make the other needlessly anxious. There is an exception to this of course; when a house is on fire, you need to mention it!

8. When you give a compliment to someone with the view of getting a favor in return.

I used this technique when I was a door-to-door vacuum cleaner salesman: give the prospective buyer a sincere compliment, and he will be more likely to buy from you. But when it comes to manipulating people to satisfy your fleshly motive, you may live to regret doing this. Whereas a little bit of sugar makes the medicine go down, we must ask ourselves: Are we playing into someone's ego in a manner that will make him do something that he will regret? If so, that person will turn on you later.

9. Being extra nice to someone of the opposite sex because they are attractive.

The thing not often openly discussed but everybody notices: the pretty face on a Christian magazine cover that has obvious sex appeal. We expect and accept this in the secular world, but this sort of thing has made its way into Christian magazines and television. A pretty face has a head start when it comes to selling magazines and books—whether in the church or the world. So you think Jesus showed favoritism to a beautiful woman? You may say: "But what is wrong with this?" I am not entering into the issue whether it is right or wrong; I am merely pointing out that we sometimes don't come face to face with our motives when God already knows what is on our minds.

10. When we defend ourselves.

The greatest freedom is having nothing to prove. When we begin defending ourselves, we are like the lady who "doth protest too much," as Shakespeare put it.[4] The last thing you and I should ever do is to vindicate ourselves. This is God's prerogative (Rom. 12:19). It is what He does brilliantly! Don't deprive Him of doing what He *loves* to do. When we begin to clear our name from what someone has said, God backs off our case. But when we turn things over to Him and take ourselves out of the picture so that He gets all the glory, He gets back on our case. At any rate, when we begin to defend ourselves from false accusations, God knows exactly what we are doing, and He is not pleased.

When we are fully aware of an audience of One, we should rethink and reconsider whether we should proceed with the thoughts in our minds. An audience of One will make all the difference if we remember that He is listening!

Chapter Three

VINDICATION

...vindicated by the Spirit.
—1 Timothy 3:16

Ye saints, who toil below,
Adore your Heavenly King,
And onward as ye go
Some joyful anthem sing;
Take what He gives,
And praise Him still,
Through good or ill,
Who ever lives.
—Richard Baxter
(1615–1691)

ONE AUGUST AFTERNOON in 1956 I fell onto a bed in my grandmother's house. I was twenty-one. I asked the Lord, "Why? How could this happen? What is going on? You promised me that You were going to use me."

Only a few months before, I was blessed with the aforementioned experience of the Holy Spirit. This experience made the person of Jesus more real to me than anybody around me. It was followed by a series of visions. I had never had a vision before, but some of these visions indicated that God was going to use me—even internationally. Until then I could not think outside the "Nazarene box." I could only think parochially—of being a Nazarene pastor. I knew that being outside my old denomination would greatly disappoint my dad. He named me after his favorite preacher, Dr. R. T. Williams, general superintendent of the Church of the Nazarene. And yet I also had a vision of my father being pleased with me.

When I came home to Ashland, Kentucky, in the summer of 1956, having resigned my first pastorate—the Nazarene church in Palmer, Tennessee—I related some of these spiritual experiences to my beloved father. My dad was the godliest man I ever knew. My first memory of him was seeing him on his knees every morning for thirty minutes before he went to work. He was not a preacher; he was a rate clerk for the Chesapeake and Ohio Railway Company. As some parents understandably do, my dad wanted to relive his life through me. He basically rejected my spiritual experiences, especially the theology they led me directly to—namely, a robust view of the sovereignty of God.

My grandmother had purchased a new 1955 Chevrolet for me to use as pastor of the Nazarene church. She took the car back.

Disappointed that my future would not be in his cherished denomination, my father said, "Son, you have broken with God." I knew he was wrong, but I could see why he thought it.

"I am closer to God than I have ever been," I insisted. Rightly or wrongly (probably wrongly), in order to impress him, I told him of some of my visions. He wanted to know *when* these visions would be fulfilled? Eager to please him, I said, "One year from now."

"Will you put that in writing?" he asked.

"Certainly," I replied. He got a sheet of paper and wrote something like, "I, R. T. Kendall, will be in an international ministry one year from now." I gladly signed my name to that statement.

That moment was painful to me. I thought my father by then would be pleased with me. A day or two later was when I lay on a bed in my grandmother's home. I was in agony, asking the Lord, "How could this happen? You promised to use me."

Hebrews 12:6 came to me. I did not know what it said. I turned to it in my King James New Testament. It read: "Whom the Lord loveth he chasteneth, and scourgeth every son whom he receiveth." That was my introduction to the biblical doctrine of chastening, or preparation. I instantly knew that God was behind my father's disappointment with me. It truly held me over the following years, but it did not eradicate the horrible pain of rejection and being misunderstood. Those were awful days.

Do you know what it is like to have vindication withheld from you? Speaking personally, it has been the source of the greatest pain of my entire life, even to this day.

From that time I lived for virtually one thing: vindication. *Vindication* means being absolved from blame or false accusation. I wanted to have my name cleared, especially with my dad. I wanted to show not only my dad but also my relatives and Nazarene friends that I had not gotten it wrong, that God was at the bottom of all that was happening.

There is more I will share. In April of that year, I heard a sermon by Nazarene General Superintendent Hugh Benner at the First Church of the Nazarene in Nashville, Tennessee. He preached a sermon from Philippians 2:5: "Let this mind be in you which was also in Christ Jesus" (NKJV). He drove home this point: Jesus had become "the lowest possible shame" for God's glory. I went to my knees and prayed: "Lord, make me the lowest possible shame for Your glory." I am not saying it was right to pray like that. But I did. The prayer was answered four months later. My entire family rejected me with one exception: Grandpa McCurley, my mother's father. He said of me: "I'm for him, right or wrong." I needed that. How sweet that was. But one close relative actually said to me, "You are a disgrace to the family."

One year after signing that paper for my dad, I was not in the ministry at all. I was working as a salesman. Five years later I was working as a door-to-door vacuum cleaner salesman. I worked as a vacuum cleaner salesman until 1967.

My father felt totally vindicated of course. Who could blame him? It was not until 1978 that my dad changed his mind. On a train from Edinburgh to London's King Cross station, my dad said to me, "Son, I am proud of you. You were right, and I was wrong." After twenty-two years I was vindicated in my father's eyes. The irony was, however, that it did not mean as much to me as I once thought it would. But at the same time I was of course pleased to hear him say this.

If only that would have been the end of an era needing vindication!

But God knew what I needed next to keep me focused on an audience of One. Withholding vindication for those twenty-two years worked so well—driving me perpetually to my knees—that the Lord apparently decided the same sort of medicine would keep working. He knows my weakness. He knows my frame (Ps. 103:14). I would need something to keep me humble and something to make me seek His face lest I take myself more seriously than I already have done. The withholding of vindication worked fairly well for twenty-two years. What might I need for the next twenty-two years? Or should I say the next forty-two years?

My answer: more of the same.

Once in a while sincere people ask me, "Would you pray for me that I can have your anointing?" These people vastly overestimate me and mean well, and I always pray for them. But I sometimes have to say that being prayed for by godly people over the years has not really worked for *me*! I have been prayed for by some of the greatest people you can imagine— from Dr. Martyn Lloyd-Jones and Billy Graham to Rodney Howard-Browne and John Arnott. Whereas I don't want to underestimate the value of these men's prayers, I have never yet *consciously* felt the slightest change or witness of the Spirit from these good people's hands on me. All I know is God has chosen a different means in my case to keep me close to Him.

It is the withholding of vindication. At almost the same time that my father's disapproval of me lifted, I began to experience the rejection of others whose disapproval, strange as this may seem, caused me greater pain than what I felt from my dad's estrangement for those twenty-two years.

It came from my Reformed friends! Disapproval came from those who embraced the theology I had come to believe.

The odd thing is that not the first Arminian, Charismatic, or Pentecostal has written a single word against me or my teaching. All my critics during my years at Westminster and since retiring from there have been those with whom I almost totally agree theologically! As Margaret Thatcher (1925–2013) once said, "It's a funny old world."[1]

These things said, you should know that my critics over the years have been godly people. Some I have known intimately, some at a distance. I can tell you, they love God as much as I do, maybe more. They believe what they uphold as strongly, sincerely, and passionately as I do. And yet their keeping a distance from me has been as painful as any grief I have ever felt during my lifetime. I know how they feel. I knew how my dad felt. I know how these Reformed men think. I am one of them! Some of them reportedly feel I stole Westminster Chapel from them. I understand this. Furthermore, my preaching for Charismatics and Pentecostals on both sides of the Atlantic has only served to convince them how far off the rails I am. Whereas the Charismatic movement in England is mainstream, in America some say it is the lunatic fringe of Christianity.

But guess what! All this has been good for me. It is exactly what I have needed. No other group on the planet would have had the slightest effect on me—much less make me turn to God for comfort. Or cause soul-searching. They have kept me on my toes. They have sharpened me. I have learned from them. Some of them are brilliant scholars and erudite writers. I look up to them. If my critics were atheists or heretics, the impact on my life would have been zero. God knows how to get our attention.

What is more, vindication from the Reformed world, although unlikely in my lifetime, would mean that God would have to find another source to keep me seeking His face. We must learn not to disdain the means God uses to refine us. It is to remind us that it is an audience of *One* that we must please. As the hymn writer Robert Robinson (1735–1790) put it, "Prone to wander, Lord, I feel it."[2] When I first started preaching, evangelist C. B. Fugett of Ashland, Kentucky, said to me, "Every compliment, every bouquet, every pat on the back resulted in no growth in my Christian life whatever, but every kick, every hurt, every criticism led to my spiritual growth." Why? Because "suffering produces endurance, and endurance produces character" (Rom. 5:3–4, ESV).

Principles of Vindication

Vindication is God's prerogative.

Over three thousand years ago God said to Moses, "Vengeance is mine, and recompense; for the time when their foot shall slip" (Deut. 32:35, ESV). (In the KJV the latter phrase reads, "Their foot shall slide in due time"—the text Jonathan Edwards used for his immortal sermon "Sinners in the Hands of an Angry God.") Deuteronomy 32:35 is quoted twice in the New Testament: Romans 12:19 and Hebrews 10:30.

It cannot be exaggerated how much God hates our trying to do His work when it comes to vengeance or vindication.

Vengeance and vindication are similar but not the same.

Vengeance refers mainly to punishment. God promised to punish sin in the Garden of Eden and did so (Gen. 2:16–17; 3:14–24). Old Testament history is a continual description of God punishing sin. God punished sin by bringing vengeance on Israel's enemies; He punished sin by allowing disobedient kings of Israel to fall. The entire sacrificial system prescribed by the Mosaic Law demonstrates God dealing with sin and showing how sin must be punished by the sacrifice of blood. God's ultimate example of punishing sin was when He punished our sins in the body of His Son, Jesus Christ (John 19:30; 2 Cor. 5:21). Vengeance is essentially God carrying out justice by punishing wickedness.

Vindication is essentially positive.

It is not always followed by vengeance. Vindication is God absolving one of blame or false accusation. For example, my dad was not punished in the slightest because he came to see that God was guiding my life over those twenty-two years he had disapproved of me. My father was thrilled. There was vindication but no vengeance.

Vindication without vengeance is equally God's prerogative.

The same principle is inflexible: whether it be vengeance or vindication, either is solely the Lord's sovereign right. He does not like it when you or I try to punish someone, to vindicate ourselves, making ourselves look good or clearing our own names. This is God's business; it is what He does.

I guarantee this: try to vindicate yourself and God will immediately get off your case. On the other hand, *let Him take over* (He doesn't want our help), and He will be on your case and do a perfect job of it. But in His time. Time is on His side. Time is God's domain.

God may choose to vindicate and bring vengeance at the same time.

A man named Korah led a rebellion against Moses and Aaron, complaining that they should share the leadership with more people than only those two men. Moses fell on his face, then said to Korah, "In the morning the LORD will show who belongs to him and who is holy, and he will have that person come near him. The man he chooses he will cause to come near him" (Num. 16:5). The next day "the glory of the LORD appeared to the entire assembly" (v. 19).

Moses put this proposition to Korah and his following:

> If these men die a natural death and suffer the fate of all mankind, then the LORD has not sent me. But if the LORD brings about something totally new, and the earth opens its mouth and swallows them, with everything that belongs to them, and they go down alive into the realm of the dead, then you will know that these men have treated the LORD with contempt.
>
> —NUMBERS 16:29–30

And as soon as Moses had finished speaking all these words, "the ground under them split apart" (v. 31). Fire came out from the Lord "and consumed the 250 men who were offering the incense" (v. 35).

This was simultaneous vindication for Moses and vengeance on those who rebelled.

After that the people continued to grumble against the leadership of Moses and Aaron. This time it was a case of vindication without immediate vengeance. Moses made this proposition: of all the twelve staffs that represented the twelve tribes of Israel, they would know God's seal of approval by which of these staffs budded. On the next day the staff of Aaron had sprouted and put forth buds and produced blossoms, and it bore ripe almonds. The fear of God fell on the people, "Behold, we perish, we are undone, we are all undone....Are we all to perish?" (Num. 17:12–13, ESV).

Vindication is sometimes immediate.

Elijah was befriended by a widow. When her son became ill and died, she turned on Elijah: "What have you against me, O man of God?" (1 Kings 17:18). Soon after that Elijah raised her son from the dead—a case of immediate vindication for Elijah. (See 1 Kings 17:17–24.) A similar event took place with Elisha, Elijah's successor—an example of immediate vindication for the prophet, with no vengeance. (See 2 Kings 4:18–37.)

When Elijah challenged the prophets of Baal, there followed both immediate vindication for Elijah and vengeance upon the wicked prophets. Upon Elijah's prayer fire fell from heaven before everybody, and the people who had been fence-straddling fell on their faces and said, "The LORD—he is God! The LORD—he is God!" (1 Kings 18:39). Elijah then ordered the people to seize the false prophets and had the prophets slaughtered, this being a case of immediate vindication *and* vengeance (v. 40).

When the apostle Paul was in Malta, a viper came out of a fire they just started and fastened on his hand. They said of Paul, "This man must be a murderer" (Acts 28:4). The people were waiting for Paul suddenly to fall down dead, but when he didn't, they quickly changed their minds and said that he was "a god" (v. 6). After that Paul healed a man with "fever and dysentery" whereupon "the rest of the sick on the island came and were cured" (vv. 8–9). This was vindication but no vengeance.

You can never figure out in advance how God will vindicate—or bring vengeance.

Take the example of Mordecai. A Jew living in Babylon during the exile of the Jews, Mordecai reported a conspiracy that would have led to the death of King Ahasuerus. Mordecai's good deed was apparently forgotten. In the meantime the king promoted a man named Haman and commanded people to bow down to Haman. Mordecai refused; he would not bow to Haman or pay homage. When I used to read this, I would say to myself, "Why would Mordecai be so stupid? What harm would it do to pay homage to Haman if it was the command of the king?" Never mind. Mordecai refused day after day. This infuriated Haman, and he tricked the king into signing a document—and sealing it with the king's signet ring—so that all Jews would be destroyed. Not only that, but Haman also erected a gallows for Mordecai to be hanged on. In the meantime Mordecai related these happenings to his close relative, Queen Esther. She knew that approaching the king without being summoned could cost her her life if the king chose. But she said to Mordecai: "Go, gather together all the Jews who are in Susa, and fast for me. Do not eat or drink for three days, night or day. I and my attendants will fast as you do. When this is done, I will go to the king, even though it is against the law. And if I perish, I perish" (Est. 4:16). During a night when the king couldn't sleep, he asked that the chronicles of memorable deeds be read to him. This was how Mordecai's saving the king's life was discovered. The king asked Haman how a hero should be honored. Thinking that the king meant Haman himself, Haman came up with rather outrageous instructions how this should be done. The king then ordered Haman to honor Mordecai with the same ostentatious recognition and asked Haman to carry it out! In the meantime the king welcomed Queen Esther. She told the king that it was Haman who caused the king to decree that Jews be destroyed. When Haman saw that his doom was sealed, he pleaded with Esther to save his life—but tripped and fell on Esther as the king entered the room. The king immediately ordered Haman to be hung on the very gallows that was made for Mordecai! (See

Esther 5:1–7:10.) Both vindication and vengeance took place in a short period of time.

The issue is the honor and glory of God. He wants *all* the glory. He is a jealous God (Exod. 34:14). As with salvation, when God gets all the glory so that we can take no credit for it, so too with vindication.

Mordecai was the hero in the Esther story. He did not raise a finger to make things happen—only to tell Esther that Haman arranged for all Jews to be destroyed. Esther got everyone to fast and pray, and God did the rest.

It is the truth that will be vindicated—not you or me.

Furthermore, only the person who has been in the right— or truly led by the Holy Spirit—will eventually be vindicated. But it is because the God of the Bible is the God of *truth*; it is impossible for Him to lie (Heb. 6:18). If you are not being vindicated, consider this: truth may not on your side after all! All of us instinctively feel that the person who has hurt us, severely criticized us, or made us look bad should be punished. But though they may be wrong to be unfair or unkind or criticize us so harshly, it does not follow that you and I are always on the side of truth. And what *you* may even regard as abuse (because you don't like the way the person spoke about you or to you) may not mean you should be vindicated. Or that vengeance should be carried out on your enemy. After all—painful though this pill is for us to swallow—our enemy *could* be on the side of truth!

If you have vindication coming, then you will get it. Eventually. God knows the truth. The truth will come out— sooner or later. It may not be in a court of law. For sometimes people get away with murder. Truth may not be seen as truth in the eyes of the majority. But God is just. He will be the

Advocate of truth and will clear your name and mine, if it is truth we are upholding, in His time.

Mark these true and faithful words:

> For there is nothing hidden that will not be disclosed.
>
> —LUKE 8:17

> Therefore judge nothing before the appointed time; wait until the Lord comes. He will bring to light what is hidden in darkness and will expose the motives of the heart. At that time each will receive their praise from God.
>
> —1 CORINTHIANS 4:5

But here is the lesson we must learn: never dismiss the possibility that the withholding of vindication is God's way of refining you! I repeat: don't despise the means God may choose to drive you to seek His face.

God loves to vindicate.

Not only is vengeance His business, but so too is the matter of vindication. He loves to do it. Don't deprive Him of demonstrating His expertise. It gives Him great pleasure. He enjoys it when we let Him do it by Himself, and I promise, He will reward you.

If you vindicate yourself—this being what most people do— it will be a hollow and temporary victory. You will eventually regret vindicating yourself. I urge you: wait.

Therefore don't deprive God Almighty of the pleasure He gets when you take your hands off and let Him work in His way and in His time. He is the expert vindicator. This is what He does. He is essentially a God of glory and justice. He does not like it one bit when one of His sons or daughters is maligned.

But at the same time—because He *is* a God of glory—He will not get involved as long as you try to help Him out. Perhaps you did not mean to rob God of glory by helping Him out, but that is what happens!

To put it another way: God is territorial. Both vengeance and vindication belong to His territory. When we move into His territory, He is not happy. "My glory I give to no other" (Isa. 42:8, ESV). He won't bend the rules for any of us. Resist the temptation to clear your name as you would avoid a venomous snake!

Take Romans 8:28, for example: "And we know that for those who love God all things work together for good" (ESV). A mistake I have made too many times is that when I have messed up by something I said or did, I hastily try to manipulate a situation and fix things quickly, only to see things get worse! Now, if it is an apology that is needed, then I must apologize. Climb down as soon as possible. And I still might have to wait a while before my mistake works together for good.

Romans 8:28 is one of the most precious promises in Scripture. It can refer to when I was in the wrong or messed up—or even when I was right but not affirmed as such. In God's time *all things* work together for good—when I was wrong or badly wrong. But God does not want my help in trying to make His promise come true! Romans 8:28 refers to our past—our pre-conversion past and our post-conversion past. All things will eventually work together for good to those who love God. Note: "love" God, not "loved" God. Romans 8:28 goes into action when we *love* Him. If we love Him, we will keep His commandments (John 14:15). Those consciously living in open sin forfeit the right to lean on Romans 8:28.

This verse does not apply to everybody; it applies to those who love God.

One more thing about Romans 8:28: the fact that something works together for good does not mean that I was right in what I did. A temptation for many of us is to claim we were in the right because things worked together for good. No! It is the sheer grace of God that makes things work together for good.

Take David's sin of adultery and murder—arguably the worst sin described in the entire Bible. But if you read Matthew 1:6— in the list of the genealogy of Jesus Christ—one might falsely conclude that it justified what David did: "David was the father of Solomon by the wife of Uriah." Oh my! Why would the Holy Spirit lead Matthew to put in those words about Bathsheba, the wife of Uriah? The answer is: *not* because what they did was right. Quite the opposite. They were grossly in the wrong. But Matthew 1:6 is an example how God turns the most evil past into good—and yet only when we love Him. Which David proved to do.

God can vindicate quickly, but vindication usually takes a good while.

Joseph foolishly told his brothers his dreams that they would one day bow down to him (Gen. 37:5–11). Telling his dreams only aggravated his brothers. It is unfair to blame his brothers for their jealousy; Joseph caused it on purpose. God made him wait a long time. The dreams were valid. The dreams were from God. There was nothing wrong with Joseph's gift. But there was a lot wrong with Joseph. He had to wait over twenty years before he was vindicated. His vindication came without vengeance upon his brothers.

The delay of vindication is an invitation from God to practice total forgiveness.

Here is why: chances are you have an enemy. An enemy may not be evil. This could merely be a person who gets your goat! Or is jealous of you. It could be someone who loves you. as my dad loved me, but who is against you in some measure. And yet, yes, it could be evil against you too. Caution: don't be hasty to call your enemy as being of the devil. People in a heated, emotional situation sometimes hastily resort to unnecessary exaggeration. Martin Luther (1483–1546) reportedly said, "Zwingli's God is my devil." What a horrible thing to say! Luther obviously wasn't perfect, but we all may be tempted to think things that are unreasonable—and articulate them.

My suggestion: behave in such a manner that the person who now seems to be an enemy will one day say to you, "You were brilliant in all that. You were great, so patient and kind." Believe it or not, today's enemy could be tomorrow's friend.

In any case, there is only one way forward when vindication is delayed: total forgiveness. And I can give you a motivation to forgive totally greater than any other that could be conceived: *you do it for an audience of One.*

Yes. That's it. That is how you do it! Total forgiveness comes easily when you realize you are doing it for God and the glory of Jesus Christ! Oh yes.

One more thing: He knows whether you are *truly* totally forgiving your enemy! You can fool me, and perhaps I can fool you, but neither of us can fool God. He knows our hearts and knows exactly what we feel and think. Why do you suppose Jesus said that we should love our enemies (Matt. 5:44)? It is because we all have them. Why do you suppose Jesus included the petition in the Lord's Prayer "Forgive us our trespasses as we forgive those who trespassed against us"? (See Matthew 6:12 and Luke 11:4.) It is because there will almost always be someone out there who will offend us in some way.

The best thing that happened to me during our twenty-five years at Westminster Chapel was being given a wake-up call from my Romanian friend Josef Tson: "R. T., you must totally forgive them; until you totally forgive them, you will be in chains. Release them, and you will be released."

Nobody had ever talked to me like that in my life. Not my parents. Not my pastors as I grew up. Not my Christian friends. Not even one of my beloved mentors. I can only say that Josef came to me at the most critical moment of my entire life. I die a thousand deaths when I contemplate where I would be today had God not sent that man to me when He did. Not only that, but what was the worst thing that ever happened to me turned out to be the *best* thing that ever happened to me (apart from my Holy Spirit experience and Louise).

This can be true with you. The worst experiences of your life can turn out to be the best things that ever happened to you, *if* you totally forgive. You let whoever sinned against you completely off the hook. You tell nobody what they did. You put them at utter ease. You refuse to cause them to feel guilty. You let them save face (instead of rubbing their noses in it). You protect them from their darkest secret. We all have skeletons in our closets. Chances are you know something about somebody that could destroy that person. Total forgiveness is when you refuse to tell what you know—and let God handle it. Moreover, total forgiveness is a life sentence; like a pill your doctor prescribes that you will have to take as long as you live, you must *keep on forgiving them*. Tomorrow. Next week. Next year. Ten years from now. The fact that you have forgiven them won't change them! By the way, you are not allowed to tell them, "I forgive you," *unless* they ask for it. The fact that you have forgiven them is a secret between you and God. Finally, you pray for them that God will *bless* them (and absolutely mean it). When you do that, you're there. For a lot more details, see my book *Total Forgiveness*.

The greater the suffering, the greater the promise of blessing for you down the road.

Suffering is "not for nothing." This is precisely why James said for us to "count it *all* joy" ("pure joy," NIV) when we fall into trials of any kind (Jas. 1:2 ESV, emphasis added). Why? Because if you *dignify the trial* rather than complain, you will see that such a trial was worth more than gold (1 Pet. 1:7).

How do you dignify a trial? Don't complain. Forgive your enemy. Maintain unfeigned thanksgiving. See the delay of vindication as part of God's strategy for you. Don't try to hasten the end of the trial. Every trial has a built-in time scale. You think it will never end? It will. When it's over, it's over. In heaven the audience of One—the righteous judge—renders a verdict of pass or fail. For too many years I failed when a trial came. I complained, grumbled, murmured, and forgot that "every joy or trial falleth from above,"[3] as the hymn writer Frances R. Havergal (1836–1879) put it. God was gracious to me, giving me many, many more chances to pass.

Has He not been gracious to you? Therefore see the withholding of vindication as the weapon He could be using to drive you to your knees to spend more time with Him. God likes your company!

Dignifying a trial is like money in the bank. It is the best investment you can make. And the greater the trial, the greater the promise of blessing—anointing of the Holy Spirit—to you.

This is the way you can discover that the worst thing that ever happened to you was the best thing that ever happened to you!

Vindication by the Spirit is the best way forward.

How do you suppose our Lord Jesus Christ was, and is, vindicated? He was "vindicated by the Spirit" (1 Tim. 3:16). His vindication was *internal*.

There are two kinds of vindication: external and internal. External—the kind we all naturally want—is when everybody congratulates you. They say, "You were right; they were wrong." Wow. What a good feeling! But really? Perhaps it is, in a sense. But that is not the way Jesus was vindicated. The Pharisees did not say, "Jesus, we think You are wonderful." The Sadducees did not say, "You are truly the Messiah." The scribes did not say, "You are the Son of God." Herod did not say, "Thank You for performing a miracle for me so that I now see who You are." Pilate did not say, "I will never sentence a man like You."

Vindication by the Spirit is a secret vindication. It is between you and God. If God gives you vindication by the Spirit, you should be the happiest man or woman on the planet. Think about it. It is when the Most High God witnesses to you in a definite and undoubted manner that *you please Him*. It doesn't get better than that.

The question is, Which gives you more satisfaction: when God pleases you or knowing that you please God? External vindication is God pleasing you—making you happy by people affirming you. And that feels good. There is no doubt about that. But there is something better than external vindication. It is the internal testimony of the Spirit that tells you in a definite and undoubted way that you are pleasing God. You are following the footsteps of Jesus.

Jesus was never vindicated externally. But He was vindicated internally by the Holy Spirit. He had the Spirit without limit (John 3:34). The voice from heaven said, "This is my beloved Son, with whom I am well pleased" (Matt. 3:17; 17:5, ESV). He said and did only what the Father told Him to say and do (John 5:19). He knew by the testimony of the Spirit that He pleased the Father. "I always do what pleases him" (John 8:29). That is how Jesus got His joy. His peace. His assurance. His confidence. He eschewed the glory from men but wanted and received the praise and glory that comes from God (John 5:44).

Jesus went unvindicated—externally—to the cross. But He went to the cross with an internal vindication.

The worst moment for Him came when God apparently turned His back on Jesus. It was when Jesus cried out, "My God, my God, why have you forsaken me?" (Mark 15:34). That was an indescribably horrible moment for Jesus. It was the only time in His life He called His Father "God." For even the internal vindication that motivated Him all His life temporarily disappeared. This happened at some point between noon and three o'clock on Good Friday. However, before He breathed His last breath, the internal vindication—fellowship with the Father—returned. He said, "Father, into your hands I commit my spirit" (Luke 23:46).

Even after Jesus was raised from the dead, He was unvindicated externally. He might have showed up at Pilate's or the high priest's door on Easter morning, "Surprise!" No. Only His faithful followers saw Him in His glorified body—those who had been *touched by the Spirit*. Not only that, but His vindication is still internal! Only those who are touched by the Holy Spirit confess that He is Lord (Rom. 10:9; 1 Cor.12:3).

Jesus' open, external, and visible vindication is in the future: it will come on the day He comes with clouds and every eye shall see Him; all peoples of the earth will "wail" when they see Him (Rev. 1:7, ESV). That is when "every knee shall bow...and every tongue shall confess" that He is Lord, to the glory of God the Father (Rom. 14:11, ESV; see also Phil. 2:9–11). Oh yes. Total vindication is coming down the road for our Lord Jesus Christ—when you and I can rejoice to see it with our eyes!

Vindication will come to you too—when the time is right. If it is delayed, it is because you aren't ready for it. "The worst thing that can happen to a man is to succeed before he is ready," Dr. Martyn Lloyd-Jones said to me. It is therefore true that the worst thing that can happen to you or me is to have our names cleared before we are ready for it.

In the meantime esteem and pursue the secret internal vindication by the Spirit. It means more than external vindication. It is worth more than ten thousand compliments from people. It is that witness that testifies, "This is the way, walk in it" (Isa. 30:21). It comes by seeking the praise that comes from God alone (John 5:44).

Chapter Four

THE GREATEST GOAL ON EARTH

How can you believe since you accept glory from one another
but do not seek the glory that comes from the only God?
—John 5:44

If you just set out to be liked, you will be
prepared to compromise on anything at any
time, and would achieve nothing.
—Margaret Thatcher

FOR REASONS I do not understand, unless it was the gracious persuasion of the Holy Spirit, John 5:44 gripped me from early on in my ministry. Over sixty years ago my old friend Billy Ball used to quote two verses all the time:

> Ye are they which do justify yourselves before men; but God knoweth your hearts: for that which is highly esteemed among men is abomination in the sight of God.
>
> —LUKE 16:15, KJV

> How can ye believe, which receive honour one of another, and seek not the honour that cometh from God only?
>
> —JOHN 5:44, KJV

These two verses are alike in three ways:

1. They are addressed to the Jews generally, but especially the Pharisees.

2. They relate to seeking approval of men vis-à-vis the approval of God.

3. They show the real reason that the Jews missed their Messiah two thousand years ago.

It was the fear of man that lay behind Israel's greatest error of all time. How true it is that "fear of man will prove to be a snare" (Prov. 29:25). The word *snare* means a trap, usually referring to catching birds or animals. But the snare of being motivated by the fear of what people think can cause human beings—even an entire nation—to be trapped and come to ruin.

The fear of man is deadly. And yet it is so ridiculous; it is worthless. The consequences of ceding to the fear of man are invariably counterproductive. Here is my favorite line from one of my favorite hymns, "Go, Labor On":

> Men heed thee, love thee, praise thee not;
> The Master praises; what are men?[1]
>> —HORATIUS BONAR (1808–1889)

I consider it a mercy from God that John 5:44 gripped me long ago. I cannot suggest for a moment that I have measured up to this very high standard, but this verse has nonetheless never been far from my thinking.

John 5:44 poses a question. It is helpful to remember that when God asks questions, He is not looking for information. The question to the Pharisees has no simple or direct answer. "How can you believe since you accept glory from one another but do not seek the glory that comes from the only God?" There is no answer, but the implication is sobering: you *cannot* believe—you are *unable* to believe—when you opt for earthly approval rather than God's approval.

Here is the question that you and I must ask: How important is God's praise to us? Or does the praise and approval of people mean more to you and me than God's praise?

Although the jealousy of God is often explicitly referred to in the Old Testament (Exod. 20:5; 34:14), do not forget we are talking about the same God. The God of the Old Testament is the God of the New Testament. The God of the Old Testament is Jesus' heavenly Father. Jesus never apologized for the things His Father did in the Old Testament, and neither must we.

It is the concept of the jealousy of God that lies behind John 5:44. God is not pleased when we let the fear of man come before the fear of God. That is what this verse means.

People sometimes ask me, "How could the Jews be so blind that they missed the very Messiah promised to them?" Good question. But Jesus' question to the Jews answers that and tells you exactly why they missed Him: *the fear of man*. Jesus wept over the city of Jerusalem because of it, knowing that the Jews were forfeiting what would have brought them peace: they did not "recognize the time of God's coming" to them (Luke 19:44).

But this verse is equally relevant to you and me today. There is a grave principle that lies behind John 5:44; it not only shows how Israel missed their Messiah but also shows how you and I can miss what God is in *today*. This is therefore an eternal principle. Jonathan Edwards taught us that the task of every generation is to discover in which direction the sovereign Redeemer is moving, then move in that direction. If we are addicted to the approval of people, we quench the Holy Spirit; it is perhaps the quickest way to put out the Spirit's fire (1 Thess. 5:19). Quenching the Spirit leads to the sad fact that we *would not even recognize* it if God were at work today. I would hate to think of the possibility that God could be at work before my very eyes and yet I miss Him entirely because I feared what people would say! John 5:44 shows the reason we may forfeit hearing God speak and consequently forfeit receiving the knowledge of God's will.

The ability to hear God's voice is a most precious asset, arguably the most precious asset you and I have. This ability to hear God speak is exactly what Israel lost when God swore in His wrath that they would not enter His rest. They became stone-deaf. Unteachable. Unreachable. It is why the writer of Hebrews quoted Psalm 95:7 in Hebrews 3:7–8, 11: "Today, if you hear his voice, do not harden your hearts as in the rebellion.... So I swore in my wrath, 'They shall not enter My rest'" (NKJV). The writer was addressing Hebrew Christians who were already "dull of hearing" (Heb. 5:11, ESV). The worst scenario would be for them to become stone-deaf like the ancient Hebrews. This explains Hebrews 6:4–6; that if these Christian Jews ended up repeating the error of ancient Israel, it would be impossible for them to be restored again to repentance. I go into considerable detail on this in my book *Are You Stone Deaf to the Spirit or Rediscovering God?* (It is a verse-by-verse exposition of Hebrews 5:14–6:20). In a word: the people described in Hebrews 6:4–6 are saved, as were those ancient Israelites, but they lose their inheritance (also called reward, prize, or crown in the New Testament). They are among those who will be saved as through "fire" but lose their reward at the judgment seat of Christ (1 Cor. 3:14–15).

John 5:44 shows the basis on which one receives a reward at the judgment seat of Christ. "For we must all appear before the judgment seat of Christ, so that each of us may receive what is due us for the things done in the body, whether good or bad" (2 Cor. 5:10). All Christians—you, me, Paul, Peter—will stand before God; some will receive a reward; some won't. The reward, as noted above, is the same as prize, crown, and inheritance. It is noteworthy that receiving a reward was very important to Paul. "I discipline my body and keep it under control, lest after preaching to others I myself should be disqualified" (1 Cor. 9:27, ESV) or "disqualified for the prize." I am of course not anyone's judge, but I have never thought it to be a very spiritual statement when one says, "I don't care about a reward at the judgment seat of Christ; I just want to make it to heaven." I say to such people: you won't feel that way then! The day you and I are called to stand before Jesus Christ the righteous judge will be the most fearful day of our lives.

John 5:44 shows that there is a difference between seeking God's praise and consciously receiving it. We may or may not consciously achieve His praise, but we can keep on seeking it. The Pharisees made no effort to do this! The question follows: Can we consciously receive His praise in *advance* of the judgment seat of Christ? Maybe, as I will show later in this chapter. I cannot forget this parable of Jesus:

> Suppose one of you has a servant plowing or looking after the sheep. Will he say to the servant when he comes in from the field, "Come along now and sit down to eat"? Won't he rather say, "Prepare my supper, get yourself ready and wait on me while I eat and drink; after that you may eat and drink"? Will he thank the servant because he did what he was told to do? So you also, when you have done everything you were told to do, should say, "We are unworthy servants; we have only done our duty."
>
> —LUKE 17:7–10

This parable leaves no room for us to think God is going to give us a pat on the back each time we do something that He has commanded us to do. This parable removes all ground of entitlement. This tells me therefore that we are commanded to seek the glory that comes from the only God—on and on and on—without knowing in the meantime to what extent He is happy with us. I choose to believe that He *is* pleased—I am sure that He is. But the honor, praise, and glory that is implied in John 5:44 is only guaranteed at the judgment seat of Christ and not before.

THE IMPORTANCE OF FAITH

Several years ago Rabbi David Rosen of Jerusalem and I wrote a book together, called *The Christian and the Pharisee* (his choice of title). These are letters that go back and forth to each other. My aim: to see him come to Jesus. His aim: to show why he does not believe in Jesus. In an early chapter he said that Israel does not really have a concept of "faith." He graciously stated otherwise when I quoted Genesis 15:6 and Hebrews 2:4 to him. But his lack of understanding of faith totally mirrored the spiritual condition of Israel in Jesus' day but also in our day. Jesus knew that Israel did not have faith. Their condition degenerated to a consensus that salvation was totally by works. As Paul put it, "For, being ignorant of the righteousness of God, and seeking to establish their own, they did not submit to God's righteousness" (Rom. 10:3, ESV). This is why Jesus put the question, "How can you believe, when you receive glory from one another and do not seek the glory that comes from the only God?" (John 5:44, ESV).

Genesis 15:6 says, "And he [Abraham] believed the LORD, and he [God] counted it to him as righteousness" (ESV). This verse became the apostle Paul's Exhibit A for his teaching of justification by faith alone apart from works. Israel missed this entirely. Not only that, but Habakkuk 2:4—"the righteous person will live by his faithfulness"—is the answer to the eternal question, "Why does God allow evil when He is all-powerful and could stop it?" Answer: we live by faith, fully believing that God will clear His name one day. This was what Habakkuk embraced and climbed down from his complaints:

> Though the fig tree does not bud and there are no grapes on the vines, though the olive crop fails and

the fields produce no food, though there are no sheep
in the pen and no cattle in the stalls, yet I will rejoice
in the LORD, I will be joyful in God my Savior.

—HABAKKUK 3:17–18

What is more, Habakkuk 2:4 is quoted three times in the
New Testament. Two of these quotes pertain to justification
by faith alone apart from works (Rom. 1:17; Gal. 3:11). The
third is Hebrews 10:38, the context showing that those who
wait on the Lord to come must rely on His faithfulness—"he
who promised is faithful" (Heb. 10:23). It further demonstrates
that Habakkuk 2:4 means that we live by God's faithfulness—
in other words, faith in God's faithfulness. I bring this out in
more detail in my book *Totally Forgiving God*. Not that God
has anything to answer for, but because we must believe in
His faithfulness and therefore set Him free to clear His name
in His own time.

God decreed that people will please Him only by their *faith*.
Faith is God's idea. No man or woman would have thought
of this. God considered "wisdom" as an option by which
people might please Him. But no. "In the wisdom of God the
world through its wisdom did not know him." God turned
that option down. But rather, "God was pleased through the
foolishness of what was preached to save those who *believe*"
(1 Cor. 1:21, emphasis added). In other words, God decided
that people would believe Him by accepting and relying on
His *word*.

The Jews in Jesus' day, especially the Pharisees, did not have
faith. They believed only in works and what would make them
look good to people. Therefore only *works* would make them
look good. For example, their righteousness—such as giving to
the poor—would never be carried out privately. Oh no! It had

to be seen! They would hire an orchestra to play when they gave to the poor (Matt. 6:1–4). The same was true regarding prayer; they prayed to be seen of men (vv. 5–6). They fasted only to be seen of men (v. 16). Jesus summed up the religion of the Pharisees: "Everything they do is done for people to see" (Matt. 23:5). In other words, they *lived* for the praise of men. As Christians we *live* by our faith in God's faithfulness to keep His word. Sadly the notion that we should seek the approval and praise of God never entered the Pharisees' minds. It was not remotely on their radar screen to seek after the praise and honor of God. *But it should have been.* Had the nation of Israel been governed by the jealousy and fear of God, they would not have missed their Messiah when He came.

It is a sober reminder that we will not always have the privilege of faith. Have you ever paused to thank God for the privilege of faith? Faith is believing without seeing. Secular atheists say they believe when they *see*. That is what those who crucified Jesus said to Him: "Let this Messiah, this king of Israel, come down now from the cross, that we may *see and believe*" (Mark 15:32, emphasis added). "See and believe"—that is the order that the atheist demands of God. But if we *see*, there is no room for faith! "Faith is the assurance of things hoped for, the conviction of things not seen" (Heb. 11:1, ESV). If you *see* something, you don't need faith.

But God requires *faith*.

Remember this too: one day the atheist will get his or her wish to see in order to believe:

> "Look, he is coming with the clouds," and "every eye
> will see him, even those who pierced him"; and all

peoples on earth "will mourn because of him." So shall it be! Amen.

—REVELATION 1:7

Picture this: people everywhere—the intellectuals, the simple, the aristocrats, the poor—crying out, "I believe. I believe. I believe." Yes. But such belief cannot be called faith when it was because of seeing. The countless billions will literally see Jesus. The same Jesus who was crucified. The same Jesus who rose from the dead. Yes. That same Jesus. Every eye will see Him. They will believe then, but such belief is not graced with the title *faith*. Faith—to be faith—is when you believe God's *word*.

You will not always have the privilege of faith. Thank God for it now. Thank God for the privilege of *pleasing* Him by faith.

GOD OBSERVES ALL OUR THOUGHTS

God is observing the thoughts and ways of men and women day and night. As we saw in my introduction, He listens to our conversations:

> Then those who feared the LORD talked with each other, and the LORD listened and heard. A scroll of remembrance was written in his presence concerning those who feared the LORD and honored his name.
>
> —MALACHI 3:16

When we all get to heaven, we will be amazed how literally true this verse is. Let this grip you. The Lord listens. Conversations with one another. The Lord is right there in the middle of us as we speak. With your friends. With those who are not real friends. With your husband. With your wife. He pays attention to every word. He hears us. Not only that, but a book of remembrance was written before Him of those who feared the Lord and esteemed His name. He examines our ways. I often quote a this verse from Jeremiah—I don't think we can hear it too often:

> The heart is deceitful above all things, and desperately sick; who can understand it?
> —JEREMIAH 17:9, ESV

But the very next verse says:

> I the LORD search the heart and test the mind, to give every man according to his ways, according to the fruit of his deeds.
> —JEREMIAH 17:10, ESV

Combine that with this verse:

> Every way of a man is right in his own eyes, but the LORD weighs the heart.
> —PROVERBS 21:2, ESV

Let me quote again my least favorite verse in the Bible—Jesus' words:

> But I tell you that everyone will have to give account on the day of judgment for every empty word they have spoken.
> —MATTHEW 12:36

God has an opinion of our thoughts and motives. As a matter of fact, He has an opinion on everything! He has an opinion on every matter. The issue is, Do we *want* His opinion? Or are we too threatened by it? Wisdom is getting God's opinion. The glory of God is His opinion. The Greek word for *glory* is *doxa*—praise, glory. The root word for *doxa* means opinion. If we get God's opinion and honor it, we will not mess up but say and do the right thing! Never forget that this wisdom is not for the person with a high IQ or with a lot of education, but it begins with the fear of the Lord (Prov. 1:7; 9:10). We all can have true wisdom.

GOD WANTS TO SHOW HIS APPROVAL

John 5:44 is given to us in Scripture that we might be motivated to want His approval more than that of people. If God did not want to show His approval, Jesus would never have said this. The truth is God wants to show us that He approves of us. It may not be a "well done" every time we do the right thing, as we saw above from the parable in Luke 17:7–10. But He nonetheless wants to show us that He is pleased, and He does so.

"How?" you will ask. The answer is: if we seek His approval because we want His glory primarily, He is happy to give us encouragements from time to time.

You will ask: Is it OK if we like it when people compliment us and show their approval? The answer is: if you did not go looking for it and it comes without your seeking it, I am sure that God delights in blessing us by sending someone to encourage us.

On one of the darkest days of my life, when I was *so* discouraged, I opened a package that was delivered to us. It came precisely at a moment—within seconds—of the time I was extremely distraught. I had been on my knees, begging God to give me some relief. I opened the package; it was from

Dr. James Dobson. In it was a copy of his book *When God Doesn't Make Sense*. Not only did Dr. Dobson dedicate the book to me, he also gave me credit in the book for one of my insights. A year before, I shared with him a thought on the issue of why God allows suffering. He seemed very grateful. I asked him *not* to quote me in the book lest I be seeking the praise of people. I meant that. But when he went ahead and affirmed me, I found out about it on the day, in the very hour of a most severe trial, and I knew God was pleased to give me a hint of His approval of me. It meant the world to me—not so much Dr. Dobson's kindness, which of course I appreciated, but God making this happen at that moment.

The greatest joy in the world is the knowledge that God approves of us. There is absolutely nothing like it, nothing to compare with it. And if what God may give us at times below is like that, I cannot but ask, Whatever will it be like when we hear from the lips of Jesus Himself: "Well done"?

Sadly the Jews forfeited that knowledge. They did not pursue it, as we saw in Romans 10:3. But the worst consequence was that they were not able to see that Jesus Christ of Nazareth was the promised Messiah that the prophets had foretold over the previous centuries. If we too follow the Pharisees, we will not only not get God's approval, but we also will miss what God may want to do in the world today. For if we opt for the praise of people rather than the praise of God, we cut off the opportunity of receiving His praise. For He is a jealous God. If you and I prefer the praise and opinion of people, we relinquish the privilege of receiving God's praise.

You possibly noticed above that the King James Version of John 5:44 refers to the honor of "God only." Most versions translate it "the only God." Either is fine. But I have always been grateful in my heart that I was trained to believe that John 5:44 not merely refers to the fact that there is but one true God but also implies we must seek the praise of God "only," that is, His glory *alone*. I am sure that this translation led me again and again to seek His praise alone and not that of people, although I have violated this a million times.

ARE THERE STEPS WE CAN TAKE?

How do we get His approval? Are there steps we can take to get it?

First, tell Him you want His opinion or approval.

Second, ask Him to show you His opinion.

Third, learn to disdain—eschew—the approval of people lest you forfeit God's approval. Don't let their praise sink in. Refuse to take it seriously. Yes, God may give you people's praise if you did not seek it. But how you handle it is of crucial importance. A person's character is revealed not only by how one handles criticism but also how one handles praise.

Fourth, try your best to get in touch with your real motives. Ask, Why am I saying this? Why am I doing this? Is it for people to notice? Am I doing this to impress people? To make them admire me? To make them jealous? Or is it for an audience of One?

What if no one is impressed with your decision? Or what you say? The question to ask is: Is *God* impressed? I think of Paul's words in his final epistle, days before his execution in Rome:

> At my first defense, no one came to my support, but everyone deserted me. May it not be held against them.
> But the Lord stood at my side and gave me strength,

> so that through me the message might be fully pro-
> claimed and all the Gentiles might hear it.
>
> —2 TIMOTHY 4:16–17

The issue then is this: what pleases Him is that you want His approval, whether or not any human being applauds you.

HOW IS HIS APPROVAL OR PRAISE MANIFESTED?

I do not guarantee all that I say at this point. I say this cautiously and guardedly. This is because the parable of Luke 17:7–10 removes all sense of entitlement or expectation of God's praise in the here and now. That said, just possibly the following might be your lot.

He lets you receive praise from people when that was not your aim. Caution: when you make this your aim, you are no longer operating for an audience of One!

He may give you the witness of His Spirit that you have pleased Him. Before Enoch was translated, he was "commended as one who pleased God" (Heb. 11:5). Commended by whom? I suspect it was the testimony of the Spirit (see Heb. 11:5, KJV). Caution: if you experience this, beware of a temptation to take yourself seriously, to feel a sense of entitlement and self-righteousness. Read Jeremiah 17:9 again!

There may be an increased measure of His anointing on your life. I know from personal experience that if I hold a grudge and do not forgive, my supply of the Spirit is, simply, shut down. But when I forgive, apologize, and become willing to admit that I was wrong, the Spirit of God returns in an undoubted manner.

There may be a time—it doesn't happen every day—in which

there is an advanced token of God's vindication here below. God may vindicate some of His children in the here and now. I have known this to happen. This is why Paul said, "Therefore judge nothing before the appointed time; wait until the Lord comes. He will bring to light what is hidden in darkness and will expose the motives of the heart. At that time each will receive their praise from God" (1 Cor. 4:5).

Whereas this verse primarily refers to the final day, it is possible that the Lord may come to step in before that day and make clear His opinion on some matters.

The ultimate and final approval of God will be revealed at the judgment seat of Christ (2 Cor. 5:10). That is what matters in the end of course. It is worth waiting for. Said Paul, "I consider that our present sufferings are not worth comparing with the glory that will be revealed in us" (Rom. 8:18).

It comes down to one thing: Do we do what we do and say what we say for an audience of One?

Chapter Five

INTEGRITY

Many claim to have unfailing love, but a
faithful person who can find?
—**Proverbs 20:6**

You're betraying your whole life if you
don't say what you think.
—**Charles Krauthammer (1950–2018)**

I T IS IMPOSSIBLE to define *integrity* adequately with one word. Typical definitions begin with *honesty* and then list other virtues: uprightness, trustworthiness, righteousness, and honor.

I read an article in the London *Daily Telegraph* as I was writing this chapter that deals with the issue "What is a Tory?" There is a philosophy in England called Toryism. It is based on a British version of traditionalism and conservatism that upholds the supremacy of social order as it has evolved in the English culture throughout history. Hence they have the Tory party. Winston Churchill (1874–1965) was a Tory. Margaret Thatcher was a Tory. But according to this article, not everyone in the Tory party is a *true* Tory. "There will never be absolute agreement on a definition," Charles Moore wrote.[1] Its elements include a disposition to conserve, a sense of history, but the concept remains "elusive." But then Moore said, "You know it when you see it," adding, "I would claim to be able to spot a Tory at twenty paces, though I couldn't tell you quite why."[2]

I think that article partly demonstrates how to explain what integrity is and who has it: you would know it when you see it. We may speak of a person who is the real deal, one who is twenty-four karat gold.

It's been said that integrity is doing the right thing even if no one is watching. And yet it is sometimes possible to demonstrate integrity when everyone is watching! For example, you may be required to be vulnerable before people if the audience of One is leading you in an undoubted but special way. What if pleasing the Lord is contingent upon our willingness and courage to be vulnerable?

Question: What if you lost your reputation simply by being obedient to the will of God? Are you willing for this?

I wish I could say that I was motivated by integrity to invite Arthur Blessitt to preach at Westminster Chapel. I cannot make that claim. Had we been enjoying a successful ministry in 1982 with the chapel filled from top to bottom, it would not have crossed my mind to invite Arthur. As they say, "You can always tell a successful man, but you can't tell him much." But when one is feeling less than successful, as I was feeling, one becomes not only more teachable but open to options one would not otherwise have been open to. That is partly why I was willing to have him.

As it turned out, then, the most crucial decision I ever made was to invite Arthur to spend the month of May 1982 at Westminster Chapel. I asked him to do the Sunday night preaching; I would do the Sunday mornings. Never in my lifetime had I been so keen to invite anybody to preach for me. I felt I understood the phrase—possibly for the first time—"fire shut up in my bones" (Jer. 20:9). The burden that was on my heart to persuade Arthur was on me from head to toe and to my fingertips. I knew it could be costly. It was. Before I invited Arthur, I had twelve deacons who supported me to the hilt. There was a wonderful unity in the chapel. After I invited him, *six of the twelve* deacons turned against me. From May 1982 until January 1985—and beyond—we were in the greatest upheaval in the history of the chapel, and I myself in the middle of the greatest testing I had ever known. Those were horrible days.

To be candid, I had no idea that Arthur would do what he did:

1. Get Westminster Chapel to sing choruses as well as hymns.

2. Give an invitation for people to confess Christ publicly—a procedure that was unprecedented in the chapel.

3. Get the people out on the streets to witness to whomever might be in our paths.

It is difficult to say which of these three changes was the most offensive. One of the deacons honestly admitted to me that it was singing choruses that upset him. Others felt I was going against Dr. Martyn Lloyd-Jones when I invited people to come forward after preaching an evangelistic sermon. The Doctor never did this, believing as he did that giving an appeal was usurping the work of the Holy Spirit. And yet the hardest decision of all was when I knew that God was calling me to start a ministry of witnessing to the lost in the streets of Buckingham Gate and Victoria. Until then my chief aspiration (I am truly ashamed to admit) was to become a world-class theologian so I could defend my view of John Calvin (1509–1564) against the traditional interpretation of him. But when I gave in to starting this street ministry, as a great hymn put it:

> Though the way seems straight and narrow,
> All I claimed was swept away;
> My ambitions, plans and wishes
> At my feet in ashes lay.[3]

I never looked back. I have never been sorry. It was indeed a *test* of my integrity—whether I would do what I *knew* I had to do before the Lord if I was to live with myself, not to mention pleasing Him not man. Possibly next to accepting Josef Tson's warning, "R. T., you must totally forgive them," a word that changed my life and lead to my book *Total Forgiveness*, inviting Arthur was the best decision I made at Westminster Chapel in twenty-five years.

Jesus said, "Whoever acknowledges me before others, I will also acknowledge before my Father in heaven. But whoever disowns me before others, I will disown before my Father in heaven" (Matt. 10:32–33). Paul said, "If you confess with your mouth the Lord Jesus and believe in your heart that God has raised Him from the dead, you will be saved" (Rom. 10:9, NKJV).

This is what I had to do publicly in my ministry—give up traditions that kept people in their comfort zones. When we do what we do for an audience of One, it is still sometimes carried out in the open in order to let the world see what God is requiring of us. I now had to do what I did as minister of Westminster Chapel. It could not be done in a corner. This is partly what made it such a test. I knew I would be questioned by some traditional Westminster Chapel supporters; I was changing some of their cherished traditions.

The truth is I never went against Dr. Lloyd-Jones at all. I always gave an invitation after he preached for me at Lower Heyford, Oxfordshire, during the three years I was a pastor while a student at Oxford University. He said to me afterward, "The way you do that, I have no problem with at all." I did not pressure people; I was merely giving people an opportunity to do what they wanted to do, not what they didn't want to do. I never—ever—pressured people but invited them to confess publicly what was in their hearts.

There was a time in ancient church history when confessing Jesus as Lord sent a signal to the authorities that made you a marked man or woman. Saying, "Jesus is Lord," was taken as an insult to Caesar, and those who confessed Jesus as Lord were liable to a martyr's death. Baptism was the ancient way of confessing Christ openly.

Josef told me that in Romania during the days when that nation was behind the so-called Iron Curtain, anyone who raised his or her hand to confess Jesus Christ in a public meeting after the gospel was preached was immediately noted by the authorities who were there to spy. Josef told me that the act of baptism some days later in those days was anticlimactic; the real test came when a person raised his or her hand in front of the crowd. It required integrity and courage.

YOU HAVE ONLY ONE LIFE

The late Dr. Charles Krauthammer, a psychiatrist who decided to become a journalist, won the Pulitzer Prize as a columnist with the *Washington Post*. I watched him on television whenever I could. I don't know if it was intended as a throwaway comment—"You're betraying your whole life if you don't say what you think"[4]—but knowing a little bit about him as I did, his words gripped me like I had not been stirred for a long time. His statement smacked of rare integrity. Here was a quadriplegic Jew, with an intellect that comes around once in a generation, who revealed why his position on various issues clearly was unmotivated by a political party or personal gain. There was no one else like him; you could not ascribe a label to him or box him into a political corner. He differed with nearly everyone day after day. It showed he was prepared to sacrifice his *whole life* for what he believed. There is no evidence that I know of that he was a believer; he was a product of God's common grace, demonstrating an unparalleled honesty that puts many a professing Christian to shame. Dr. Krauthammer apparently realized that his life had been spared for a purpose, and he was prepared to live out that purpose by an astonishing integrity and was not going to waste it by appealing for approval from those around him.

"Whole life." Think about it. You have only one life. You will have only the one body you now have. The one mind and will you now have. Therefore your entire life is on the line by what you say and do. Not to speak up for what you believe in your heart of hearts is a betrayal of your whole life.

Jackie Pullinger, who has become a legend in her own time because of her ministry in Hong Kong, said something similar to what Krauthammer said, except that she believes in heaven: "We are going to feel stupid for eternity if we waste this life."[5] I know what she means by that. Oh yes, God will wipe away all tears (Rev. 21:4), no doubt about that. But at the same time, at least when we stand before the judgment seat of Christ to give account of the things done in the body, whether good or bad (2 Cor. 5:10), we will have cause to regret with incalculable sorrow if we have not found our niche to live for God's glory on this earth.

Jesus said, "Whoever wants to be my disciple must deny themselves and take up their cross and follow me" (Mark 8:34). By that Jesus meant that we must be willing to lose *everything* for Him. But only if you really do believe that He is the Son of God who died on the cross for your sins and was raised from the dead. You either believe that or you don't. As C. T. Studd (1860–1931) put it:

> If Jesus Christ be God and died for me, then no sacrifice can be too great for me to make for Him.[6]

And if you do believe this, said Jesus Himself, you must not remain in hiding. You must "acknowledge" ("confess," KJV) Him before men (Matt. 10:32). You have to come out into the open, in front of everybody.

Joseph of Arimathea was a man of wealth and prestige. He was a secret disciple of Jesus. In other words, he was in hiding but believed that Jesus was authentic. Real. The truth. Perhaps he waited too long to come out of hiding; Jesus was now a dead man on a cross. But when there was nothing to gain, he openly asked Pilate if he could take the body of Jesus down from the cross. Permission granted. It was too late to confess Jesus—as he might have done while Jesus was still alive. He did the next best thing: he knew he would betray his whole life if he did not take a stand for Jesus. Even if Jesus were dead. There was no future in doing this. Joseph had everything to lose, nothing to gain. But he knew he would betray his whole life if he did not say what he thought—that Jesus really was the Son of God. Joseph was prepared to lose everything by taking the body of Jesus down from the cross *in front of everyone.*

Compare Joseph's unusual courage with that of the twelve disciples. The disciples of Jesus figured they had a great future by following Him. They were convinced He was Israel's Messiah. So much so that James and John lobbied to be front and center in Jesus' coming kingdom (Mark 10:37). But when the pressure was on and the authorities were closing in on Jesus, Judas Iscariot betrayed Him (Matt. 26:14–16), and Peter denied Him (vv. 69–74); indeed, "all the disciples deserted him and fled" (v. 56). In a word: the disciples had a brilliant future but forsook Jesus.

Joseph of Arimathea was not promised any benefit by coming out of hiding after Jesus was dead and confessing his true sentiments about Him. But by his extraordinary decision to ask for the body of Jesus, Joseph showed he had integrity. He would rather blow away his own future by telling the world what he believed about Jesus than let the opportunity to identify with Jesus pass him by. It was a last-ditch effort to say, "Yes, I am a follower of Jesus." He got in under the wire, just in time to bear the stigma.

Have you ever thought of the importance of a stigma? It is hugely important. The value in a stigma—assuming it is the right kind—is inestimable. It is worth more than a million diamonds. The opportunity to embrace a genuine stigma does not come around every day. But when you discern that a valid kind of stigma is on offer, grab it. Leap to get it. Take it with both hands. It will demonstrate before heaven that you are doing what you are doing for an audience of One.

The word *stigma* is a pure Greek word. It means to stick or prick.[7] In Hellenistic literature it was described as a tattoo on the bodies of runaway slaves, who would be "marked." The most natural, sensible, and intelligent decision in the world would be to avoid a stigma as you would avoid drinking poison. But if the right kind of stigma comes your way, namely, suffering for the glory of Christ, its value is of greater worth than any commodity in this life. A wrong kind of stigma would be suffering as a thief, murderer, or meddler. Or from any foolish decision. But if you are "insulted because of the name of Christ, you are blessed, for the Spirit of glory and of God rests on you" (1 Pet. 4:14). Mind you, part of the stigma often comes from respectable people who question whether the decision you made was wise. They may say you were foolish! And that pretty much gets to the heart of what makes a stigma a stigma.

A good definition of *stigma* is *whatever causes embarrassment* when you throw your reputation to the wind for the sake of maintaining integrity.

The irony is that Peter, in a dark moment of his life, showed no integrity. It was when he denied knowing Jesus (Luke 22:54–62). He was not only forgiven by Jesus (v. 32) but was even chosen to preach the inaugural sermon of the church on the day of Pentecost (Acts 2:14–36)! This goes to show how God forgives us for the sin of not showing integrity! We've all been cowards at one time or another. But God gives us a second chance, as he did to Peter. That is what makes bearing a stigma sweeter than honey.

Question: Do you know what it is not to show integrity? Have you ever been a genuine phony? And then felt ashamed? Have you said to yourself, "God can never use me now that I have let Him down like that?" Be of good courage. Peter wept bitter tears for his caring more about his reputation than he did the honor of Christ. I suspect he said to himself, or even prayed to God, "Give me one more chance."

He got it. He and John were summoned to appear before the Sanhedrin. They were beaten and charged not to speak in the name of Jesus. I can imagine that those pompous Pharisees and Sadducees said, "Well, that will show them. We taught them a lesson." No. The truth is Peter and John could not believe their luck (if I may be forgiven for using that word) that they were *privileged* to bear this stigma. They left the presence of the council "rejoicing because they had been counted worthy of suffering disgrace for the Name" (Acts 5:41), "suffering dishonor" (ESV), "suffer shame" (KJV).

Think about this! They now regarded *shame for the name* an honor.

If you have shown lack of integrity in your past and are

truly sorry, I would urge you now to ask the Lord to give you a second chance! Be ready for it! And when it comes, seize upon it with all your strength. Remember Romans 8:28: "All things work together for good to them that love God, to them who are the called according to his purpose" (KJV).

Consider the prophet Jonah. God told him to go to Nineveh to preach. Jonah said, "No." God then said, "Really?" He sent the wind and arranged a big fish to swallow him to get Jonah's attention (Jon. 1–2). Jonah prayed for a second chance. A gracious God came to him "a second time: 'Go to the great city of Nineveh'" (Jon. 3:1–2). Jonah prayed to get to do what he initially refused to do—and God answered him with a big yes.

God will do this for you too.

As for Joseph of Arimathea, he actually knew in his heart that he was not blowing away his future by confessing Jesus. He was "waiting for the kingdom of God" (Luke 23:51). This tells me that the Holy Spirit was at work in Joseph. He believed that Jesus would be raised from the dead! It was not blowing away a future after all but getting into the kingdom of God while faith could be truly *faith*. He believed so deeply that he went out into the open in front of anybody who happened to be there to identify with Jesus Christ.

Integrity is revealed by what you will give your whole life for. And living for an audience of One. Lack of integrity is exposed by caving into the fear of man.

I preached my first sermon at the Calvary Church of the Nazarene (the building has since been torn down) in Nashville, Tennessee, on December 2, 1954. It was on the faithfulness of God, my text being Lamentations 3:23: "Great is thy faithfulness" (KJV). In the sermon I quoted Proverbs 20:6. "Most men will proclaim each his own goodness, but who can find a faithful man?" (NKJV).

The greatest hurts of my life have sometimes come from some of the people I admired—probably admiring them too much—who, so it seemed to me, did not show integrity when I needed them. Every person I have known that I began to admire a little bit too much, sooner or later disappointed me. This is not their fault. It is mine. One should know not to admire anyone too much. The best of men are men at best. I hate to think it, but I am sure there is someone out there who has been hurt by me.

God is faithful because He is a God of integrity. In Him there is no guile, no guilt, no shame, no injustice. He cannot lie; He keeps His word (Heb. 6:18; Titus 1:2). Likewise Jesus, the Son of God, mirrors His Father's integrity and faithfulness. This is why Paul could say, "I live by the faith [or faithfulness] of the Son of God" (Gal. 2:20, KJV, with my translation from the Greek). God keeps His word; He will never let you down.

That said, if you and I are to maintain integrity, it means we must reflect the character of God, namely, trustworthiness, honesty, graciousness, and faithfulness.

MODESTO MANIFESTO

In 1948, before he became very famous, Billy Graham and three friends—Cliff Barrows (1923–2016), George Beverly Shea (1909–2013), and Grady Wilson (1919–1987)—felt the need to make a covenant with each other. They were aware of so many people in the ministry who went off the rails in various ways. They had the perspicacity to see that this could happen to them. In a hotel room in Modesto, California, they covenanted together to maintain certain principles. They called it the Modesto Manifesto. These principles came under four areas:

1. *Money.* The four men were aware that some evangelists emphasized money a lot and spent time taking love offerings. They vowed never to emphasize money. They would also let someone else handle the money. Local campaign committees would oversee the offerings and the distribution of funds. They also agreed to live on a certain salary, no matter how much the offerings increased in their campaigns.

2. *Sexual purity.* A number of religious leaders, especially those who traveled, were falling into sexual sin. The men agreed to pray continually to God that they would be kept from this. They set up some rules. They would never allow themselves to be alone with a woman— whether at meals, counseling sessions, or traveling. I had the privilege of knowing each of these men except Grady Wilson. But I did know his brother, Thomas Walter Wilson (1918–2001), who like me went by his initials. T. W. took Grady's place when he died. T. W. became the "shadow" of Billy Graham. Billy never stayed in a hotel room alone; T. W. was always in the same room.

3. *Criticism.* Some evangelists openly criticized local pastors from pulpits. The men vowed not to do this, nor would they criticize those who criticized them.

4. *Exaggeration.* The phrase *evangelistically speaking* has been coined to label exaggerated figures of the number of people attending meetings or the number of people who came forward to confess Christ publicly. The men vowed to be honest in this matter. If numbers were mentioned, they came from information from the local police, fire departments, or arena managers.[8]

Best of all, these men kept their vows! Did it pay? Oh yes. I doubt that *any* public figure has been scrutinized like Billy Graham or members of his team. The world tried to get something on them, but they never did. Graham and the other men kept their covenant with each other. There is no doubt in my mind that God honored Billy Graham, part of the reason being these principles laid down in what years later Burrows called the Modesto Manifesto.

"The integrity of the upright guides them, but the crookedness of the treacherous destroys them" (Prov. 11:3, ESV). It is my opinion that people with a big hole in their integrity will be found out. "Be sure your sin will find you out" (Num. 32:23), whether in this life or at the judgment seat of Christ. "Whoever walks in integrity walks securely, but whoever takes crooked paths will be found out" (Prov. 10:9).

You don't need to read far into Proverbs until you see the connection between the fear of the Lord and wisdom, integrity, and sexual purity. The beginning of wisdom is the fear of the Lord (Prov. 9:10). One fruit that one who fears the Lord must desire is that he or she will maintain sexual purity. This is why you have—almost in your face—repeated warnings about adultery, the immoral woman, and sexual promiscuity early on in Proverbs, as in Proverbs 5, 6, and 7. An earthly fruit of the fear of the Lord will be wisdom. How important is wisdom? "Love her, and she will watch over you....Cherish her, and she will exalt you; embrace her, and she will honor. She will give you a garland to grace your head and present you with a glorious crown" (Prov. 4:6–9).

David resolved before the Lord: "I will walk with integrity of heart within my house" (Ps. 101:2, ESV).

INTEGRITY IS NOT FOR SALE

It is often said that *every man has his price*. Really? Can *you* be bought off? There are stories of spies, whether with the KGB, the CIA, or MI6, who have crossed over to work for the enemy they started out to be against. Why? They had a price. They could be bribed. It has happened with corrupt judges, politicians, those who worked for their government. It has happened with men and women who went to Hollywood—aspiring to become a star—who succumbed for a price. I'm afraid that there are those in the ministry who traded their convictions for the invitation that promised a high honorarium.

Elisha—The Syrian commander, Naaman, came to Israel to be healed of leprosy by Elisha. Assuming he would need a lot of money, the wealthy general brought silver and gold and other commodities that would be worth millions today. He was not prepared for the kind of person that would be healing him. First, Elisha did not even come out to meet Naaman. That was a humbling moment for the Syrian general. Generals are used to everybody bowing and scraping before them. Second, he was told by Naaman's servant to dip himself in the Jordan River seven times. That was even more humbling. But he finally yielded, did what he was told to do, and was miraculously healed (2 Kings 5:14). After that he meets Elisha for the first time. Naaman is overwhelmed with the miracle and wants to show his appreciation and gratitude to the prophet Elisha. Elisha almost certainly lived on the offerings of people. But when a wealthy Syrian shows up, Elisha won't take any money at all. Elisha wanted to teach Naaman a lesson—that the God of Israel is different from the gods of Syria. "As surely as the LORD lives, whom I serve, I will not accept a thing" (v. 16). Naaman was given a glimpse of sheer grace. The glory of God meant more to Elisha than anything else.

However, Elisha's servant Gehazi was of a different ilk. As we will see again and further below, he chased Naaman's caravan before he got too far and lied to Naaman, saying that Elisha had changed his mind and would take a gift after all. Of course, said Naaman. Gehazi should have known better. Elisha perceived Gehazi's wicked deed by the Spirit, and the result was that Gehazi was struck with leprosy for the rest of his life—and also lost his job. But there is an aspect of the story that moves me more deeply; Elisha does not command Gehazi to go and tell Naaman the truth. This would seem to be a natural thing for Elisha to do—to make sure that Naaman did not believe that Elisha put Gehazi up to what he did. But Elisha did nothing. He did not even bother to protect his own reputation with Naaman; he let him think whatever he willed.

This to me is amazing. Elisha knew that *God* knew the truth.

Even though Elisha wanted to teach Naaman a lesson, namely, to let Naaman see what the God of Israel is like, Elisha still did not try clear his name before Naaman.

All Elisha did was for an audience of One. That is what mattered to Elisha—that God Himself knew. Elisha wanted the praise that comes from God only (John 5:44).

It hurts a lot when people believe things about you that are not true. Especially if those who love, support, and admire you are told things that are not the truth. The temptation can be heavy to say something! Tell the world the truth! But to do that would be forfeiting the praise that God would have given, not to mention risk losing the anointing. It's not worth it to try to clear your name! That is why I admire Elisha so much.

LOYALTY TO GOD AND HIS WORD

Abraham—Sometimes God asks us to believe and do things that make no sense at the time. God "tested" Abraham and said to him:

> Take your son, your only son, whom you love—Isaac—
> and go to the region of Moriah. Sacrifice him there as
> a burnt offering on a mountain I will show you.
> —GENESIS 22:2

This is arguably the strangest, most apparently unfair, and most seemingly senseless request of God to be found in the entire Bible. This command of God makes no sense at all. First, why sacrifice Isaac? It would have made more sense for God to sacrifice Ishmael since he was a "child of haste" (as in my book *Believing God*). Ishmael became Abraham's idea when he went along with Sarah to lay with her servant Hagar to make good God's promise to Abraham.

Second, Abraham believed the Lord when He promised Isaac to him and Sarah in their old age. Indeed, Abraham:

> ...did not weaken in faith when he considered his own body, which was as good as dead (since he was about a hundred years old), or when he considered the barrenness of Sarah's womb...but he grew strong in his faith, as he gave glory to God, fully convinced that God was able to do what he had promised.
>
> —ROMANS 4:19–21, ESV

Third, God made it clear to Abraham that Isaac, not Ishmael, was to be the promised child (Gen. 17:18–21). That said, why ever would God ask Abraham to sacrifice Isaac?

Amazing. Extraordinary. It made no sense at all.

Here is what is even more extraordinary: Abraham obeyed! He followed through. He knew two things full well:

1. God gave him Isaac.

2. Isaac was the only link to the fulfillment of the promise that his seed would be as the sand of the sea and the stars of heaven.

Did Abraham complain? Did he say, "Why, Lord?" One would sympathize had Abraham done so. But in his own mind Abraham reckoned that God would raise Isaac from the dead (Heb. 11:19). In other words, Abraham knew two things: his own seed would be as the sand of the sea, and that Isaac was the promised seed. That is how much he believed God's word!

His own reasoning was, simply, that he must sacrifice Isaac and then wait for God to raise him from the dead.

But God had another idea. The moment Abraham was about to come down with the sword and slay his beloved Isaac, God stopped him! "Do not lay a hand on the boy....Now I know that you fear God, because you have not withheld from me your son, your only son" (Gen. 22:12).

It was Abraham's finest hour. He not only showed complete loyalty to God and His word but was rewarded with God swearing an oath to him (Gen. 22:16; Heb. 6:17).

Abraham did not question God's word. He got it wrong by thinking that God would raise Isaac from the dead.

Abraham should be your role model—and mine. It means believing God's word even when it makes no sense at the time.

Here's the thing: God always honored the person who held to Scripture. "You have so exalted your solemn decree that it surpasses fame" (Ps. 138:2). King Saul became "yesterday's man" (as in my book *The Anointing*) because the scripture that stated that only the person called of God should offer the burnt offering made no sense to him. Through Moses the Lord had said:

> No one except a descendant of Aaron should come to
> burn incense before the LORD, or he would become
> like Korah and his followers.
> —NUMBERS 16:40

Saul was an outsider in this case. King of Israel, yes. But an outsider when it comes to burning incense before the Lord. Only the person called of God could do this. And because it made no sense to him, Saul, feeling justified, went ahead and offered the burnt offering (1 Sam. 13:9). It cost him everything

(1 Sam. 13:13–14). In case you think this was a mere one-off incident and should not be taken too seriously, you should know that the great king Uzziah made the same mistake. He too burned incense on the altar. Uzziah was warned, "It is not right for you, Uzziah, to burn incense to the LORD." The result was that Uzziah was struck with leprosy. He was a leper to the day of his death (2 Chron. 26:18–21).

You and I face the same thing. There are passages in the Bible, Old Testament and New Testament, that don't make sense to us. It will be to our folly if we dismiss these merely because they don't make sense to *us*—as if our opinion is valid and lets us off the hook because we deem ourselves capable of judging God's Word. Never forget that the Bible is God's integrity put on the line. He knows what He has written. He has not forgotten what He has written. His Word is a *test* whether we will believe His Word or dismiss it because it does not make sense to us.

As Paul put it, "Who are you, a human being, to talk back to God?" (Rom. 9:20). Who do we think we are, that we can judge God Almighty?

The best thing I ever heard Rick Warren say was when he was being interviewed a few years ago by John Piper. Rick said that when he came upon a scripture that he did not understand, he always attributed it to his own lack of knowledge rather than the integrity of the Bible.[9]

The Bible is God's integrity put on the line. God magnifies His Word above all His name! That is what the Hebrew says in Psalm 138:2, which the King James Version translates literally: "Thou hast magnified thy word above all thy name."

I can think of nothing more wonderful, nothing more consoling than this: the God of the Bible is a God of pure integrity. The same can be said about His Son.

Chapter Six

THE INTEGRITY OF JESUS

———◆———

Teacher…we know that you are a man of integrity
and that you teach the way of God in accordance
with the truth. You aren't swayed by others,
because you pay no attention to who they are.
—MATTHEW 22:16

Integrity is the glue that holds our way of life together.
We must constantly strive to keep our integrity intact.
When wealth is lost, nothing is lost; when health is lost,
something is lost: when character is lost, all is lost.
—BILLY GRAHAM (1918–2018)

BEHOLD THE MAN!" said Pontius Pilate (John 19:5, ESV). What a sight it was. Pilate stated these words to the crowd of Jews demanding that Jesus be crucified. Jesus had been forced to wear the crown of thorns and a purple robe (John 19:5). What a moment to be witnessed by the Jews—but also by the angels and sainted dead in heaven looking on. The crown of thorns was placed on Jesus both to humiliate Him and to make Him suffer. The purple robe put on Him was to make fun of Him—purple being the color of royalty. Since Jesus claimed to be a king, they provided this robe for him. It was the ultimate effort to embarrass Him as well as to inflict physical pain.

How did this make Jesus feel—feeling the pain and the humiliation before the people? Answer: He hated it. He despised the shame. Yet He gladly dignified this suffering for at least two reasons:

1. Since it was carried out before an audience of One—His Father.

2. Knowing the joy that was set before Him (Heb. 12:2).

Knowing that this was part of the will of the Father for Him, the pain and humiliation was worth it all. Pleasing the Father gave Him more satisfaction than any amount of pain relief, even if such relief had been available or on offer. The joy of pleasing the Father transcended all His suffering. The greater the anointing, the greater the suffering. Jesus had the ultimate anointing that ever was or ever will be. Jesus suffered more than anybody ever did or ever will.

The next time you suffer the slightest bit of embarrassment

over what you stand for, remember that it is a small price to pay if it results in a greater anointing. It might also mean that in your case God has already decreed a greater anointing for you and that, if so, humiliation is always an essential part of the package. Furthermore, the next time you suffer physical pain—for whatever reason—remember that your suffering does not even come close to the pain Jesus suffered.

Do you want a greater anointing? Really? Are you sure? The anointing is like wisdom or understanding: "though it cost all you have," get it (Prov. 4:7). And it will cost you! *This is because it comes with pain.* This is why James urged us to count it "pure joy" when we fall into any kind of testing or trial (Jas. 1:2). The Greek word *peirasmos* means temptation, trial, or testing.

In the days we were being led out of our comfort zone in Westminster Chapel, one of our deacons—a very posh and gentry-bred one—asked, "Do we really want revival?" He was admitting that he was very uncomfortable with changes that needed to be made. Indeed, the greatest trial of my whole life was in the years 1982–1985 when six of our twelve deacons tried their best to get me fired. We survived. But those were hard days. When the storm finally passed by, I said: "Never again will I go through this. I have proved I was willing to lose everything. But no more risks for me." But God said, "Really?" Would you believe that I had to do it all over again? Yes. I have learned that there is basically one way to keep from becoming yesterday's man—namely, the willingness to keep going outside one's comfort zone.

The anointing of the Spirit comes with a price: integrity.

It is impossible to know exactly what was on Pilate's mind when he said, "Behold the man." Was it to call attention to the fact that Jesus was the focus of what the fuss was all about? This would mean that Pilate was merely stating, "Here's the man you Jews are so upset about." Or was it because Pilate was impressed with the amazing character of Jesus, seeing the way He coped so valiantly and calmly during this ordeal? Paul referred to the "good confession" Jesus made before Pilate (1 Tim. 6:13). Or did John quote Pilate in order to call attention to Jesus' humanity? One of the most interesting things about the Gospel of John is that it shows with equal emphasis the truth about Jesus' deity and humanity. The Word, who was God (John 1:1), was made flesh, showing He was fully man (v. 14).

I can understand that the world cannot accept the truth that Jesus was and is a man who was and is God. But there have always been those Christians who struggle to believe He really was and is a *man*! Nobody knows who wrote the Apostles' Creed or when it was first drawn up (possibly in the second century). There are different translations, but this one is possibly the most common:

> I believe in God the Father Almighty, maker of heaven and earth, and in Jesus Christ, His only Son, our Lord, who was conceived by the Holy Spirit, born of the Virgin Mary, suffered under Pontius Pilate, was crucified, dead, and buried. He descended into hell; the third day He rose from the dead. He ascended into heaven, and sitteth at the right hand of God the Father Almighty. From thence He will come to judge the quick and the dead. I believe in the Holy Spirit, the holy Catholic [universal] church, the communion of saints, the forgiveness of sins, the resurrection of the body, and the life everlasting. Amen.[1]

The Apostles' Creed was actually written in order to demonstrate that Jesus was truly human—a literal man. It was drawn up to refute the ancient gnostic heresy that Jesus was not truly a literal human being but only appeared to be a man. Hence the Apostles' Creed was drawn up to defend that Jesus *was and is* truly a *man*. Note the words from the creed: Jesus was "*born* of the Virgin Mary, *suffered* under Pontius Pilate, was *crucified, dead*, and *buried*" (emphasis added).

Question number forty-one in the Heidelberg Catechism (1563) asks: Why was Jesus buried? Answer: to prove He was truly dead. It was a miracle that He *died*. The death of Jesus was as great a miracle as His resurrection. Think of this: Jesus—God—died. He actually died. Isaac Watts (1674–1748), in his immortal hymn "Alas! and Did My Savior Bleed," uses the phrase "When Christ, the mighty Maker died."[2] Or as Charles Wesley (1707–1788) put it, "Amazing love! How can it be, that Thou, my God, shouldst die for me!"[3]

I remember when 1 Timothy 2:5 first gripped me: "There is one God and one mediator between God and mankind, the *man* Christ Jesus" (emphasis added). It was when the greatest experience of my life took place—when the Holy Spirit filled me and brought me face to face with the reality that Jesus *was and is* truly a man—a literal man, a human being. Knowing that He was truly God, I remember being astonished and amazed how truly human Jesus was and is. He was just like us; He was tempted and tried like we are but without sin (Heb. 4:15).

God's eternal decree regarding the plan of redemption required that Jesus was truly to be a man in order to be our *substitute.* He took our place—in life and death (Rom. 5:10). In what sense are we saved by Jesus' *life*? Answer: He did everything for us that is required of us. He kept the Law for us (Matt. 5:17). He was baptized for us in order to "fulfill all righteousness" (Matt. 3:15). He believed for us (Rom. 3:22, KJV; Gal. 2:16, KJV; Heb. 2:17). He did *everything* as our substitute. Then when He died, His blood satisfied God's justice and wrath, this blood being a "propitiation" for us (Rom. 3:25, KJV). *Propitiation* means that Jesus' blood turned God's wrath away from us. Jesus did this as a man. The justice of God was totally and eternally satisfied by what Jesus did for us—in His life and by His death.

JESUS AND THE AUDIENCE OF ONE

Jesus as a man was the perfect example of a person who lived totally and utterly for an audience of One. All that Jesus ever said or did was for the glory of the Father. "I do not seek my own glory" (John 8:50, ESV). "I seek not my own will but the will of him who sent me" (John 5:30, ESV). When the Pharisees said to him, "You do not care about anyone's opinion, for you are not swayed by appearances" (Matt. 22:16, ESV), they were trying to flatter Jesus so that they could trap Him. Jesus of course saw right through them; He could see they were even patronizing Him. He overlooked it. But in stating what they did, they spoke the absolute truth: Jesus was not the slightest bit influenced by people's opinions, prestige, or connections. He could not be swayed or bribed.

We know that Jesus was tempted at all points just as you and I are, but we don't know what kind of temptation was the most difficult for Him to resist. He was no doubt tempted by the devil to eat when He was on a fast in obedience to God, but He resisted the thought of turning stones to bread as He could have done (Matt. 4:3–4). The temptation to hunger was a physical temptation. The temptation regarding the sexual desire also refers to a physical need. He was also tempted to put God to the test by throwing Himself down from the pinnacle of the temple (vv. 5–7). And He was tempted by Satan to accept the glory of the kingdoms of this world, but He said, "Away from me, Satan!" (vv. 8–10). It was this third test that would border on the issue of the honor of God only. It would seem that resisting this temptation set the stage for His living entirely for an audience of One—His Father.

The temptation to live for the approval of people is possibly what mostly challenges one's decision to live for an audience of One. Was Jesus truly tempted to live for the praise, approval, glory, and honor from people? Of course He was. This is why He can sympathize with us. "Because he himself suffered when he was tempted [or tested], he is able to help those who are being tempted" (Heb. 2:18). An extraordinary truth is Jesus learned obedience through suffering (Heb. 5:8). If the sinless Son of God learned obedience by what He suffered, how much more do we—frail children of dust—need suffering to bring us to obedience to Christ?

Never forget that all that Jesus said or did was directed in heaven from the Father. Indeed the character of Jesus mirrors the character of His Father. The words of Jesus originate with the Father. No wonder, then, that Jesus could say, "Anyone who has seen me has seen the Father" (John 14:9). There is perfect unity between the Father and the Son. "I and the Father are one" (John 10:30).

DID JESUS WORRY
ABOUT HIS REPUTATION?

There is a paradox here. When it came to the opinion of the Pharisees, He did not care about His reputation. He saw a man called Matthew sitting at the tax booth and said to him, "Follow Me." Matthew did so. Not only that, but "many tax collectors and sinners came and ate with him and his disciples." The Pharisees asked Jesus' disciples, "Why does your teacher eat with tax collectors and sinners?" (Matt. 9:10–11). It was a frequent criticism: "The Pharisees and the teachers of the law muttered, 'This man welcomes sinners and eats with them'" (Luke 15:1–2).

This kind of criticism did not bother Jesus the slightest bit. He replied in two ways. First, by saying, "Those who are well have no need of a physician, but those who are sick" (Matt. 9:12, ESV). "I have not come to call the righteous, but sinners to repentance" (Luke 5:32). Second, by three parables: the parable of the lost sheep (Luke 15:3–7), the parable of the lost coin (vv. 8–10), and the parable of the prodigal son (vv. 11–32). Each of these show God's love for the lost sinner.

Jesus was merciless toward the self-righteous, the hypocrites, and the Pharisees. He poked fun at those who only give to the poor to be seen—having trumpets play to attract a crowd when they gave to the poor (Matt. 6:2–4). All they do is done for men to see, said Jesus (Matt. 23:5). He noted that these people pray in synagogues "to be seen by others" (Matt. 6:5). Furthermore they fasted in a manner that called attention to their fasting: they "look somber" and "disfigure their faces to show others they are fasting" (v. 16).

The religion of the Pharisees was the polar opposite to what Jesus wants of His followers: to give, pray, and fast not for people to know but for an audience of One. As for giving, "do not let your left hand know what your right hand is doing." In other words, there is a sense in which we *do not even tell ourselves* when we give. This way, "your Father, who sees what is done in secret, will reward you" (Matt. 6:3–4). When you pray, "go into your room, close the door and pray to your Father, who is unseen" (v. 6). Likewise with fasting: make sure your fasting "will not be obvious to others...but only to your Father, who is unseen" (v. 18).

The paradox of Jesus' concern for His reputation is demonstrated when He chose to pay taxes when He would not have had to. He did not want to give needless offense. His critics asked His disciples whether their teacher would pay the two-drachma tax. Jesus explained that He did not have to pay taxes; kings don't pay taxes. It was an implicit admission that He was a king. (See Matthew 17:25–26.) But so as to "not cause offense, go to the lake and throw out your line. Take the first fish you catch; open its mouth and you will find a four-drachma coin. Take it and give it to them for my tax and yours" (v. 27). Whereas Jesus did not protect His reputation with the Pharisees, He was careful not to give "offense" regarding innocent people who may not understand. This shows not only Jesus' acknowledgement that He was a king but also His care for sincere people who might be unnecessarily puzzled by His refusal to pay taxes.

All of us must learn from this. This is why Paul showed his wisdom concerning eating meat that may have been sacrificed to idols. Whereas there is nothing in such meat that is "unclean in itself," it is nonetheless unclean for anyone who, "regards something as unclean." Therefore if your brother is grieved by what you eat, "you are no longer acting in love" (Rom. 14:14–15).

Paul also said, "All things are lawful for me," but "not all things are helpful" (1 Cor. 6:12, ESV). "Therefore, if what I eat causes my brother or sister to fall into sin, I will never eat meat again, so that I will not cause them to fall" (1 Cor. 8:13).

Should you and I care about our reputations? Sometimes yes and sometimes no. Yes, when it comes to hurting another's conscience. We need to be seen as humble and caring for the weaker Christian. A good name is of considerable worth and such honors God (Prov. 22:1). But we should certainly *not* worry about our reputations when it comes to personal pride.

Did you ever think that Jesus was sometimes rude? Consider this passage:

> A Canaanite woman from that vicinity came to him, crying out, "Lord, Son of David, have mercy on me! My daughter is demon-possessed and suffering terribly." Jesus did not answer a word. So his disciples came to him and urged him, "Send her away, for she keeps crying out after us." He answered, "I was sent only to the lost sheep of Israel."
>
> —MATTHEW 15:22–24

Does this sound like the Jesus you have admired? Does this sound like the same Jesus who said earlier: "Come to me, all who *labor* and are *heavy laden*, and I will give you rest....I am gentle and lowly in heart" (Matt. 11:28–29, ESV, emphasis added)? This poor woman was very distressed indeed! Not only that, but what might people who are looking on now think of Jesus! Did He not care how He must have appeared to such onlookers?

Of course He cared. But He cared more about the audience of One—what the Father thought.

There is more to the scenario of the Canaanite woman, however. Jesus gave but a temporary impression of rudeness. As it happened, the distraught woman persisted and demonstrated such earnestness and faith that Jesus was touched and answered the woman's request:

> The woman came and knelt before him. "Lord, help me!" she said.
>
> He replied, "It is not right to take the children's bread and toss it to the dogs."
>
> "Yes it is, Lord," she said. "Even the dogs eat the crumbs that fall from their master's table."
>
> Then Jesus said to her, "Woman, you have great faith! Your request is granted." And her daughter was healed at that moment.
>
> —MATTHEW 15:25–28

Jesus might have appeared rude when someone said to him, "Teacher, tell my brother to divide the inheritance with me," and Jesus responded, "Man, who appointed me a judge or arbiter between you?" (Luke 12:13–14). In this case Jesus simply refused to get involved in a family quarrel. But it shows that He does not mind cutting across wishes that we may have. If He were overly concerned by appearing to be rude, lest He be criticized, He would have said more. But He was concerned not about what people thought but about seeing and hearing the Father.

He was ruthless with the Pharisees. Knowing that they did not grasp what He taught, Jesus said to them: You don't understand me because God is not your father; Satan is:

> You belong to your father, the devil, and you want to carry out your father's desires. He was a murderer

from the beginning, not holding to the truth, for there
is no truth in him. When he lies, he speaks his native
language, for he is a liar and the father of lies.

—JOHN 8:44

Whereas He had endless patience and compassion for the sinner, He was the opposite with self-righteous people. The scribes and Pharisees brought a woman caught in adultery. The Law says she should be stoned. But what would Jesus do? He said to them, "Let any one of you who is without sin be the first to throw a stone at her" (John 8:7). One at a time they walked away. He then said to the woman, noting that the Pharisees would not condemn her, "Neither do I condemn you....Go now and leave your life of sin" (v. 11).

You might say, "How could Jesus expect to win over the Pharisees when He spoke to them as He did?" The answer is that He never was trying to convert them in the first place. Not only that, but their father was the devil. His Father chose who would come to Jesus: "All those the Father gives me *will* come to me, and whoever comes to me I will never drive away" (John 6:37, emphasis added). Had they chosen to come to Jesus—as Jews like Nicodemus and Joseph of Arimathea did— they would have been accepted. Although Jesus stated that the father of the Pharisees was Satan, there were exceptions—or Saul of Tarsus would never have been saved. This obviously includes people like Joseph of Arimathea and Nicodemus.

As for Nicodemus, Jesus was impartial and unimpressed both with Nicodemus' stature and the fact that he came to Jesus at night when no one would notice. Not taken in by Nicodemus' flattery—"Rabbi, we know that you are a teacher who has come from God. For no one could perform the signs you are doing if God were not with him," Jesus came right to the point: "Very truly I tell you, no one can see the kingdom of God unless they are born again" (John 3:2–3).

Would you be willing to talk like that to a highly prestigious person? Would you be so overcome by his fame and importance that you would be afraid of offending him or missing out on getting to be seen with him that you forget the gospel? We are commanded to share the gospel will *all* people—rich, poor, famous, unknown, Jews, Gentiles, Muslims, and Mormons.

Jesus was even very willing to be misunderstood. This is in contrast to those of us who might panic at the thought of someone misunderstanding us. When Jesus said, "Destroy this temple, and I will raise it again in three days" (John 2:19), He knew of course how this would go down with His opponents. The Jews then said, "It has taken forty-six years to build this temple, and you will raise it in three days?" (v. 20). Jesus made no reply. The Jews used this statement against Him before the high priest (Matt. 26:60–61). It was John who wrote the fourth Gospel many years later and gave the explanation: "But the temple he had spoken of was his body. After he was raised from the dead, his disciples recalled what he had said. Then they believed the scripture and the words that Jesus had spoken" (John 2:21–22). But Jesus did not bother to explain this!

In somewhat the same way, Jesus put off thousands of His followers when He said that to follow Him meant they must eat His flesh and drink His blood! They said, "This is a hard teaching. Who can accept it?" (John 6:60). Did Jesus panic at this? Did He say, "Oh dear. Sorry I did not explain what this means. I am only talking about a sacrament that will be called the Lord's Supper later on"? No. He said nothing.

Jesus was not running for office. He was not trying to build up a following. In fact, when thousands wanted to make Him king, He quickly got away from the crowd to be alone (John 6:15).

And yet Jesus was equally impartial regarding those followers closest to Him. When Peter confessed, "You are the Christ, the Son of the living God," Jesus affirmed him: "Blessed are you Simon Bar-Jonah! For flesh and blood has not revealed this to you, but my Father who is in heaven." (Matt. 16:16–17, ESV). But moments later Jesus rebuked the same Peter soundly. When Jesus explained that He must be killed and on the third day be raised, Peter took Jesus aside—as if to give the Lord some necessary advise. Peter actually rebuked Jesus! He said. "This shall never happen to you!" Jesus' reply to the same Peter who had been affirmed earlier was "Get behind me, Satan! You are a stumbling block to me; you do not have in mind the concerns of God, but merely human concerns" (vv. 21–23).

Integrity must likewise be manifested sometimes with those we know best, those closest to us, and who may support us.

Jesus never gave *anyone* a feeling that he or she could somehow have a claim on Him. As I quoted previously from one of my earliest mentors Dr. N. Burnett Magruder: "The only evidence that I have seen the Divine Glory is my willingness to forsake any claim upon God." I have taken many years to absorb this and apply it. It is true. And Jesus never allowed people to get so close to Him that they might think that they could control God or tell Him what to do! Jesus would not "entrust himself" to the crowds generally, because He knew what was "in each person" (John 2:24–25), nor would He allow anyone to think they were so close to Him that they could demand things of Him.

This could be a warning to those who allow wealthy or influential people to own them (so to speak). This is a delicate

matter. Over the years I have had those followers and supporters whom I truly needed, but who clearly wanted to be in
control of me. They might not put it like that, but they didn't
need to. It was obvious. They wanted my ear; they wanted to
give me advice; they wanted very "in"; they wanted to be the
audience of one! They wanted to be closer to me than anyone
else. I remember one deacon whose advice I had to reject, and
this deacon became virtually an enemy. It hurt.

I came across a writing some sixty years ago called *The
Didache*, known as the "teaching of the twelve apostles."
Possibly written in the second century, one can get a flavor of
how Christians thought during those early times. One must
not take this writing too seriously, but I myself was deeply
struck by one line in this document. One of the ways to recognize whether a prophet was true or false was this, "If he asks
for money, he is a false prophet."[4] Oh dear.

Simon Peter sincerely believed that he was closer to Jesus
than all the rest and that he loved Jesus more than the eleven
other disciples. When Jesus stooped to wash the feet of the
Twelve, Peter tried to impress Jesus by saying, "You shall never
wash my feet." The Lord replied, "Unless I wash you, you have
no part with me." Then Peter—determined to upstage the
other disciples—said, "Not just my feet but also my hands and
my head as well" (John 13:8–9). This scenario helps explain
what Jesus meant after His resurrection when He said to Peter,
who had denied Him, "Do you love me more than these?"—
namely, these other disciples. Peter still didn't get it; that is, he
didn't see the pride and deceitfulness of his own heart: "You
know that I love you" (John 21:15). Shortly after that Jesus told
Peter how he would die: "You will stretch out your hands, and
someone else will dress you and lead you where you do not

want to go" (vv. 18–19). Peter seemed more concerned about how John would die: "What about him?" Jesus, refusing to let Peter have any claim upon Him, said, "If I want him to remain alive until I return, what is that to you? You must follow me" (vv. 21–22).

The rivalry among the early disciples of Jesus did not end with either the resurrection or Pentecost. There would be an even greater challenge for these men down the road when one "untimely born" came along, namely the apostle Paul. The conversion of Saul of Tarsus was in God's sovereign will. But it was extremely hard for these men who knew Jesus in the flesh— especially Peter and James the brother of Jesus—to accept Paul. It could have felt like a betrayal from Jesus. But the truth was none of them had the intellect of Paul, and none of them could explain God's eternal purpose and salvation by grace through faith alone like Paul. They had to make room for Paul, which Peter finally did (2 Pet. 3:15–16).

This should be a lesson to all of us today. We may feel we have a corner on some truth, that we have the franchise of a particular teaching. You may also feel betrayed that you don't have another's intellect or anointing. Or fame. I have struggled here. For this reason I have made it a personal practice for several years to read Romans 12:3 literally every day in addition to my regular Bible reading plan:

> For by the grace given me I say to every one of you:
> Do not think of yourself more highly than you ought,
> but rather think of yourself with sober judgment, in
> accordance with the faith God has distributed to each
> of you.

This verse keeps me in my place as Jesus' word to Peter was meant to keep him in his place vis-à-vis John's future (John 21:21). After all God is sovereign; it is He who gives to each of us a measure of faith. Nobody can do everything. This verse reminds me not to complain that I am no Jonathan Edwards or Martyn Lloyd-Jones.

The integrity of Jesus meant that *nobody* who followed Him got too close. Even the extraordinary conversion and deliverance of the demon-possessed man from the country of the Gerasenes did not warrant him a position with the Twelve. He begged Jesus that he might stay with Him and follow Him everywhere from then on. But no. "Go home to your own people and tell them how much the Lord has done for you, and how he has had mercy on you" (Mark 5:18–19). One of the hardest things a pastor or evangelist faces is to keep their greatest converts from feeling they have a claim of some sort— that they should inherit a special relationship.

The proof that we have truly seen the glory of God is that we will willingly forfeit any right to entitlement or claim upon the Lord. We must bow to His sovereignty to show we love His glory more than the praise of people and are not following Him for what it might do for our prestige if we have a special ministry.

The integrity of Jesus was rooted in His loyalty to the Father. He did totally nothing that would displease the Father.

I sometimes think that Jesus' finest hour was when He refused to answer Herod. Hoping he might see Jesus perform a miracle before his very eyes, Herod was pleased to meet Him. Herod questioned Jesus at some length, but Jesus' response was utter silence (Luke 23:9). The greatest freedom is having nothing to prove.

I have thought a lot about the agony Jesus felt on the cross—apart from the physical pain—when He was not permitted to explain what was going on to His convert Mary Magdalene. Mary could not figure out what was happening. How could this be—this same Jesus who walked on water and raised Lazarus from the dead would let them crucify Him? There she was, sobbing her heart out. Jesus was not even allowed to whisper to her, "It's OK, Mary. It is part of the Father's plan. I'm dying for the sins of the world." No. Part of His pain was seeing her pain when He was not permitted to say a single word.

It was for an audience of One.

But one of the most moving moments that demonstrated Jesus' integrity was when He appeared to ten of His disciples on Easter Sunday evening. These men had forsaken Jesus in the previous three days (Matt. 26:56). Peter, who was so convinced of His devotion to Jesus that he thought would never, ever deny Him, did precisely that. All these men felt dreadful. They were scared to death of the Jews. They were ridden with guilt that they forsook Jesus.

Then Jesus walked through locked doors and appeared. Whatever would Jesus say to them? Would He scold them? Moralize them? Rub their noses in it? "How could you do this to Me? I taught you over three years, spoon-fed you and let you hear all My sermons and see My miracles. How dare you to desert Me in My darkest hour?"

Did He say that? No. Instead He said, "Peace…as the Father has sent me, I am sending you" (John 21:21). Jesus practiced what He preached. Not only did He pray for forgiveness for the Roman soldiers (Luke 23:34), He maintained integrity with those who hurt Him the most. It was as if nothing had happened! Instead of saying, "I had great plans for you men, but you've blown it big time; I cannot use you now," He said, "As the Father has sent me, I am sending you."

No. The "everlasting love" (Jer. 31:3) of God was in action with these unworthy men. The least likely person to be used on the day of Pentecost was the man who was so self-righteous and confident of his loyalty but messed up—Peter himself.

The integrity of Jesus is what guarantees that you and I— with all our sin and self-righteousness—will be kept to the end. Even when we mess up.

Chapter Seven

CHARACTER AND GIFTING

He [the Father] causes his sun to rise on the evil and the
good, and sends rain on the righteous and the unrighteous.
—MATTHEW 5:45

For God's gifts and his call are irrevocable.
—ROMANS 11:29

Integrity without knowledge is weak and useless, and
knowledge without integrity is dangerous and dreadful.
—SAMUEL JOHNSON (1709–1784)

A S A YOUNG boy I idolized preachers. I got this from my
dad. He made a point of introducing me to preachers.
As I said previously, I was named after his favorite
preacher, Dr. R. T. Williams. My father introduced me to Dr.
Charles E. Fuller (1887–1968) in Long Beach, California, when
I was eleven years old. Dr. Fuller was the famed preacher of
The Old Fashioned Revival Hour and founder of Fuller Theological Seminary. Our church in Ashland, Kentucky, had three
"revivals" (missions) every year. We always had the guest evangelist have dinner with us. I met dozens of them and looked
up to them all.

One of these evangelists—Earl Savage (not his real name)—
had, it seemed, more power and authority than many of the
others. I stood in awe of his persuasiveness, boldness, and
effectiveness. I got as close to him as I could, trying to squeeze
out any bit of knowledge that would help me to have that kind
of power, should I ever become a preacher.

But I also heard some time afterward that a woman—not
his wife—followed him from town to town without anybody
knowing who she was. She would always stay in the same hotel.
This apparently went on for a long time. And then all this came
out and was relayed to the host pastor, who received this information midway during a two-week meeting in Ashland. He
kept quiet until after the final Sunday evening service was over
and then confronted this visiting preacher. Strange as it may
seem to you, many people professed conversion over the two
weeks, and that final Sunday evening seemed to be accompanied with more power and conviction than ever!

Figure that out. What is the explanation? The answer I
believe can be explained in more than one way. First, to know
what common grace is. *Common grace*, which John Calvin

called "special grace,"[1] is a wonderful gift from our Creator. Common grace is God's goodness to all men and women, saved or lost.

There are then two categories of grace:

1. *Saving grace*—given to only to those who embrace the gospel by faith.

2. *Common grace*—which all people have, with or without faith.

It is called common grace not because it is ordinary but because it is given commonly to everyone. It has nothing to do with conversion; it is a creation gift and is usually refined by upbringing, education, childhood experiences, and peer relationships. It is what gives people their IQ and their love for knowledge or a particular profession or hobby, and what may lie behind their oratorical skills. It is what produces an Albert Einstein (1879–1955), a Sergei Rachmaninoff (1873–1943), a Winston Churchill, or a Nelson Mandela (1918–2013).

Or an Earl Savage. One explanation in this case is that sincere people in my Nazarene church in Ashland had been praying for revival. They came to church with expectancy. Such sincere people may not always have discernment. God honors the prayers of His people. God used Savage's preaching ability to sway an audience and bring people to the Lord—and move people like me to want to preach like this man, should they ever go into the ministry.

Common grace. Never underestimate it. Be thankful for it. It is God's gift to humankind. The rain falls on the just and the unjust. The sun shines on good people and bad people. All of us—even the most unworthy of us—have been blessed with a measure of God's special grace in nature: one's love for music, the talent to play a violin, the genius to make money, an ability to become a rocket scientist, or the ability to be a persuasive orator when speaking in public. When a natural-born orator becomes a preacher, this person will be able to persuade an audience—whether he or she has been converted or not.

That is part of the explanation as to why famous TV evangelists excel in their gifting. It *could* be nothing but common grace at work.

However, such a scenario is not always mere common grace at work; hopefully such preachers have been genuinely converted and have the anointing of the Spirit that comes from *saving* grace. Somehow they fall into sin, and yet God continues to use them.

GIFTING AND A MORAL LAPSE

This brings me to the second point in this connection. A truly saved person may have a moral lapse and continue in his or her gifting. I choose to believe that is what happened with Earl Savage. King David was a man after God's own heart (1 Sam. 13:14; Acts 13:22). But he succumbed to sexual temptation and committed adultery with Bathsheba, wife of Uriah. David later had Uriah killed, hoping to cover up the adultery. It is arguably the worst sin described in the Old Testament. He apparently continued as an effective king until Nathan the prophet found him out some two years later (2 Sam. 12).

Therefore the Earl Savages of this world or famous TV evangelists' immorality can be explained not only by common grace but also by being a fallen saint. If it could happen to David, it could happen to you and me. This is why Paul said that if a brother is overtaken in a sin, we who are spiritual should restore such a person in a spirit of meekness, considering ourselves lest we also be tempted (Gal. 6:1). This should be a lesson to all of us: when we hear of a person falling into sin, whatever it is, we should fall on our knees and say, "There go I but by the grace of God." Otherwise it could be you or me next.

That said, there is a third explanation for the flourishing of one's gift despite one's personal character: the gifts and calling of God are irrevocable (Rom. 11:29, "without repentance" KJV). This means that a gift, once bestowed, is yours to keep, regardless of your integrity or character.

Evidence for this: King Saul. He was turned into another man—given a new heart—and was endowed with the gift of prophecy (1 Sam. 10:9–13). Later on, having become Israel's first king, he became jealous of young David. He was more fearful of David than he was of the enemy of Israel—the Philistines. Not only that, but on his way to try to kill David, his prophetic gift suddenly kicked in. Saul's gift of prophecy was so extraordinary that people said, "Is Saul also among the prophets?" (1 Sam. 19:24). Imagine that! The same Saul with murder in his heart simultaneously manifested a prophetic gift so that the people were in awe!

Does this surprise you? It may well surprise you, but I would lovingly urge you to be aware that there is more than one explanation for someone's gift dazzling people when the person himself or herself is living a double life.

These things said, the purpose of this chapter is to raise the question: Which is more important—gift or character?

There are actually those in ministry who uphold the premise that gifting is more important than character! It ought to be an issue beyond discussion; surely character is more important!

But let me put the case on behalf of those who want to champion the belief that gifting is more important than character. We are living at a time when church attendance is going down, down, down. Young people are deserting the church more, more, more. One of the reasons for the decline in church attendance is boring church services—boring preaching and boring singing and, in some cases, boring liturgy.

In comes a gifted speaker. Or faith healer. Or prophet. Crowds come to hear such a person. They are suddenly excited and want to come back and hear and see this gifted person again.

Who can blame them? I would too.

When I was at Westminster Chapel, I could guarantee that a congregation size would be doubled if I announced that the guest would be a well-known person with charisma, charm, personality, international reputation, and extraordinary gifting.

Yes. Because this is what interests people. I understand this. I would go out of my way myself to hear or see such a person. What is more, if the man's gift is truly of God, would we not want God to use this person?

I watched a well-known prophet call out from the Westminster Chapel pulpit a lady named Elizabeth and an address in nearby Pimlico. I knew the lady and the background situation, which I had told to no one. The background was this: The lady's unsaved and ailing husband, Sam, was visited by Benjamin, one of our deacons, in the hospital three nights before Sam died. This deacon led Sam to the Lord. Elizabeth was overjoyed. But a few weeks after Sam passed away, she began to wonder whether her husband had truly been converted. After all he was drugged for pain, and she began to question whether Benjamin was right to say Sam was truly saved. One day Elizabeth asked the Lord to give her assurance that her late husband was truly in heaven. She saw a Bible open on a table and walked over to it. Her eyes fell on words that referred to the Lord being with Samuel. Samuel! Yes, that was her husband's name. She was so pleased. But the next day she noticed that this was a children's Bible, and she began to doubt whether she could believe that the Lord truly gave her an affirming word about her husband.

A few days later at Westminster Chapel our visiting prophet—in the middle of his sermon—suddenly looked down at Elizabeth, calling out her name and address. She looked up with bit of astonishment. He said to her: "At this address the Lord recently met with you. But you were afraid that it wasn't really the Lord. I can tell you, Elizabeth, it was the Lord." I will never forget the look on Elizabeth's face. She was ecstatic with joy. She never doubted her husband's salvation after that.

I am relating this because I found out later that this prophet's character was deeply flawed—to put it mildly. I was saddened beyond words when I found out he was living a double life. And yet this man had been a great blessing to Westminster Chapel at a critical time. He did us no harm, and I thank God for him.

But would I invite him back again if I had a choice? No.

One might make a case for gifting being more important than character based on this story about Elizabeth and Sam. I can understand this. But such thinking goes right against New Testament teaching regarding holiness. In Paul's last letter before he was beheaded in Rome, he put it like this:

> In a large house there are articles not only of gold and silver, but also of wood and clay; some are for special purposes and some for common use. Those who

cleanse themselves from the latter will be instruments
for special purposes, made holy, useful to the Master
and prepared to do any good work.

　　　　　　　　　　　　　—2 Timothy 2:20–21

What Paul writes to Timothy challenges us to live a life for
an audience of One. The appeal to gifting over character is
based on attracting an audience of thousands.

Case closed, in my opinion.

Take John the Baptist. He performed no miracles. Indeed,
"many people came to him." The people said, "John did no
sign, but everything that John said about this man [Jesus]
was true" (John 10:41, ESV). John the Baptist had an anointing
that attracted people to come twenty miles from Jerusalem to
hear him. It was the fear of God that emanated from John's
preaching. The first message of the New Testament was by
John: "You brood of vipers! Who warned you to flee from the
coming wrath?" (Matt. 3:7). John the Baptist was fearless. He
preached holiness: "Produce fruit in keeping with repentance"
(Matt. 3:8). He was beheaded because he said to Herod, "It is
not lawful for you to have your brother's wife" (Mark 6:18, 27).
He preached Christ: "Look, the Lamb of God, who takes away
the sin of the world!" (John 1:29).

As there are two categories of grace, saving grace and
common grace, so also are there two levels of anointing—that
which flows from obedience and pleasing the Lord, and that
which flourishes because it is based on an irrevocable gift.

But cannot a person who pleases the Lord by his or her holy
life have *both*? Cannot a man of God also have such an irrevocable gift? Absolutely, if God grants it. We should pray for this
(1 Cor. 12:31). But in my opinion we should never for settle for

a gift that is not matched by sexual purity, detachment from the love of money, and true humility.

I would urge the reader of this book to covet the kind of anointing that comes from the desire to perform before an audience of One. Paul said, "In Christ we speak before God" (2 Cor. 2:17). A preacher of the gospel should imagine that he is speaking as if the Lord Jesus were consciously looking on. When a preacher knows that a famous person is in the audience, it is hard not to think of him or her. If one spoke at St. George's, Windsor Castle, one would be speaking before Her Majesty. It would be pretty hard not to think of her in preparation and delivery! And yet I suspect John the Baptist would have been unintimidated by such an audience. When Paul spoke before Felix, the subject turned from Paul's personal interest to the final judgment. As Paul spoke, Felix trembled. He was alarmed (Acts 24:25). When Paul spoke before King Agrippa, the focus was not his personal fate but the gospel—so much so that Agrippa actually asked Paul, "Do you think that in a short time you can persuade me to be a Christian?" (Acts 26:28). Absolutely, said Paul! This is why Paul stated that he would speak before an audience of One—"before God." This statement followed his comment, "We are not, like so many, peddlers of God's word, but as men of sincerity, as commissioned by God" (2 Cor. 2:17, ESV).

Paul warned us that in the last days there would be those people who turn away from listening to the truth. They want teachers "to suit their own desires." They will "gather around them a great number of teachers to say what their itching ears want to hear" (2 Tim. 4:3).

My deepest fear is that the craving for a person with gifting rather than character stems not from the love of the gospel but the desire to have a greater number of people to preach and speak to. Who can blame them? I sympathize! I prefer to preach to thousands than to hundreds. Who wouldn't? But I can also say that I would prefer to see the smile from the audience of One than the acclamation of thousands. After all it is the audience of One I shall behold on that last day. The thousands won't matter then.

Chapter Eight

THE FAITH HALL OF FAME

Therefore, since we are surrounded by such a great cloud
of witnesses, let us throw off everything that hinders
and the sin that so easily entangles. And let us run with
perseverance the race marked out for us, fixing our eyes
on Jesus, the pioneer and perfecter of faith. For the joy
set before him he endured the cross, scorning its shame,
and sat down at the right hand of the throne of God.
—HEBREWS 12:1–2

Two roads diverged in a wood, and I—
I took the one less traveled by,
And that has made all the difference.
—ROBERT FROST (1874–1963)

GENERALLY SPEAKING, THERE are two kinds, or levels, of faith: saving faith and persistent faith. Saving faith—also called justifying faith—is the faith that gets us to heaven. It comes by transferring our reliance on good works to what Jesus Christ has done for us on the cross. You may recall that in chapter 1 we saw that the blood of Jesus is a propitiation for our sins; it turns the Father's wrath away. It satisfies His justice. We get to heaven by putting all our eggs into one basket: what Jesus has done for us by His sinless life and sacrificial death.

Persistent faith is the faith of the "cloud of witnesses" described in Hebrews 11, namely, the faith of those Old Testament stalwarts who turned their world upside down by their faith. Hebrews 11 is not a description of saving faith—with the possible exception of that of Abel in Hebrews 11:4. Hebrews 11 generally describes those people who, by persistent faith and pursuing their inheritance, accomplished astonishing things.

The people of Hebrews 11 also had this in common: they lived for an audience of One.

These things said, I want to examine Hebrews 11:3:

> By faith we understand that the universe was formed
> at God's command, so that what is seen was not made
> out of what was visible.

No person of faith is named in Hebrews 11:3. Only *"we."* Who are "we"? Answer: believers—from the people of the Old Testament down to the present moment. Hopefully the "we" are you and me—that is, if you too believe that the universe was created by the word of God so that what is seen was not made out of things that are visible.

Faith Defined

Years ago I asked Dr. Martyn Lloyd-Jones for a good definition of *faith*. He thought about it and phoned me the next day: "Believing God—there's your definition." I knew then and there that was it! Faith is believing God—that is, believing what He says, believing His Word, believing the Bible.

The writer of Hebrews defines *faith* at the beginning of the chapter:

> Now faith is the assurance of things hoped for, the conviction of things not seen.
>
> —Hebrews 11:1, esv

> Now faith is the substance of things hoped for, the evidence of things not seen.
>
> —Hebrews 11:1, kjv

> Now faith is confidence in what we hope for and assurance about what we do not see.
>
> —Hebrews 11:1

Faith and Full Assurance

The Greek word *hypostasis* is translated "assurance," "substance," and "confidence."[1] The essence of true faith contains a measure of assurance. There is a difference between mere "assurance" (*hypostasis*), and "full assurance" (*plerophoria*) (Heb. 6:11; 10:22). The latter refers to the immediate and direct witness of the Holy Spirit; it is when God swears an oath.

Therefore the faith described in those people of faith in Hebrews 11 is assurance but not always *full* assurance. The difference can be summed up this way: assurance is believing

God; full assurance is believing you *have* received what you pray for, as in Mark 11:24: "Believe that you have received it, and it will be yours." It is *knowing* that you have been heard when you pray (1 John 5:15).

The faith of the people described in Hebrews 11 is that they believed God when He spoke. Faith is *believing God*, that is, believing His Word.

This is vitally important when it comes to Hebrews 11:3— belief in creation *ex nihilo* (out of nothing): "By faith we understand that the universe was formed at God's command, so that what is seen was not made out of what was visible." The issue is whether God applied matter that already existed when He created the heavens and the earth or whether He created the universe out of *nothing*. Creation *ex nihilo* is to believe that God created what is from what did not exist. It came into existence by His sheer word.

It happens that since writing the previous paragraphs, I witnessed to a taxi driver in London whose name is James. He was a true Cockney—that is, he was born within the sound of Bow bells in East London. His accent proved it, reminding one of Eliza Doolittle in the musical *My Fair Lady*. Dr. Lloyd-Jones always insisted that there is a difference between being intellectual and being intelligent. He said, for example, that an Oxford don (professor) is intellectual but a Cockney taxi driver is often more intelligent than an Oxford don. This taxi driver was a perfect example of Dr. Lloyd-Jones' distinction. At the appropriate time I began to talk to James about the gospel. When I mentioned Jesus Christ, he dismissed Him as "rubbish." He immediately said that he gave up belief in God long ago because God would surely not allow all the evil and suffering in the world. For some reason he made reference to the universe and especially to stars with their "energy."

"Where do you suppose those stars came from?" I asked him.

"That's the question, isn't it?" he replied.

I said to James, "You and I both have faith—no question about it. You have faith that matter is eternal; I have faith that God created the stars out of nothing."

"I guess that's right, isn't it," he said.

"Yes. It comes down to what your faith will do for you when it comes time to die. My faith assures me I will go to heaven. You choose to believe that there is nothing to follow death. If I am wrong, I have nothing to lose. If you are wrong, it's a pretty serious thing—eternity lasts a long time."

He went quiet. To my surprise he was shaken rigid. He even became very open to the gospel. I prayed with him and bid him farewell as we reached the destination.

Hebrews 11:3 is possibly the most important verse in Hebrews 11. Here is why. Every generation has its stigma by which the believer's faith is tested. One of the greatest stigmas of our day is belief in creation by God. There is nothing more challenging, nothing more offensive, and nothing more emotive than the premise that God created the heavens and the earth as described in Genesis. When I first preached on Hebrews 11 at Westminster Chapel forty years ago, Christians were embracing the theory of evolution in rapid numbers. But today I am sorry to say that many of the most respected evangelicals on either side of the Atlantic have espoused evolution— theistic evolution, that is, believing that this was the way God *chose* to create the heavens and the earth.

What is the problem with believing in theistic evolution? Answer: it is choosing to believe science rather than the Bible.

Instead of accepting the plain teaching of Hebrews 11:3—"by faith"—one takes his or her cue from science. Science is given priority over Scripture.

The issue is whether matter is eternal. Even some evangelicals say yes, that *matter* was always there. If that is true, creation out of nothing is out of the question. Hebrews 11:3 clearly takes the position of creation out of nothing: what is seen was *not* made of what is visible. This is because there was a time when nothing was there—but God. Jesus said He is the "first and the last" (Rev. 22:13). Had there been one speck of dust in remotest space before God created the universe, Jesus would not have been first. It is the biblical position that there was a time when there was *nothing there but God.*

But that offends people. Why? Because science says otherwise. We live in a generation that has made a choice: to believe science rather than the Bible. Sadly the number of Christians who have made that choice is increasing daily. And yet the irony is that science is always changing. Read a science book on evolution today and one from fifty years ago—they differ on many things!

What worries me is we are not listening to an audience of One when we opt for theistic evolution. We are listening to people. We are opting for the majority. It is our comfort zone; we avoid a stigma, that is, looking like fools when we say we believe in creation out of nothing.

The issue is which comes first: faith or understanding? Hebrews 11:3 says, "By faith we understand." The opposite approach is we understand, then believe. The secular view of faith is "I will believe it when I see it." That is what the people said to Jesus on the cross: "Come down now from the cross, that we may see and believe" (Mark 15:32). The biblical view of faith is we believe and then see; the worldly view is we see and then believe. But according to Hebrews 11:1, faith is believing without seeing the evidence. The atheist says, "That's dumb. That is stupid. How could anyone believe without knowing for sure what is there to believe?" But, like it or not, Hebrews 11:1 says that what makes faith *faith* is that we believe without seeing the evidence. In other words, if we believe because we have *seen*, such faith cannot rightly be called faith.

According to Hebrews 11:3, then, understanding follows faith. We don't understand first, then believe.

To put it another way, God has decreed that we accept creation *ex nihilo* because we choose to believe God. If science were suddenly to decide unanimously to embrace creation as told in Genesis and then we believe it, it would not be faith anymore. Science proving Genesis eliminates the possibility of faith. Had Jesus come down from the cross and the priests and soldiers immediately said, "I believe! I believe!" it would not have been faith at work. It would have been sight. In the same way, if all the scientists reject evolution and accept the Genesis account, it would rule out faith; it would be by sight.

It is *God* who has said we are to accept creation out of nothing *by faith—by believing Him.* He is a jealous God. If we believe creation *ex nihilo* because science says it is now safe to believe in creation *ex nihilo*, this would not honor Him. He wants us to believe His Word.

I was a student at Southern Baptist Theological Seminary in the days when most of the faculty not only did not believe in Jesus' literal resurrection from the dead, but they praised Charles Darwin (1809–1882), although most scientists have since moved way beyond Darwin. They believed in evolution and in the higher criticism of the Bible, as particularly championed by men like Rudolf Bultmann (1884–1976). There were thankfully some exceptions but not many. My main theology professor—whom I was personally fond of and who recommended me to the Faculty of Theology at Oxford University—said, "I went from fundamentalism to the theology of Karl Barth. I then went from Barth to Paul Tillich. From Tillich to process theology. And now I don't know what I believe." Those were his very words.

I can tell you how this could happen in a seminary, especially my old seminary in Louisville, Kentucky. It is because they wanted to impress the theologians of Harvard, Princeton, and Yale. By embracing much of German theology, they demonstrated they were scholars of world class—which is what they wanted. In other words, they would be praised as truly learned—equal to anyone on the planet. The praise and glory of man. Sadly that was more important to them than pleasing an audience of One.

Belief in creation by faith is what will please the audience of One. You will be popular in heaven but stigmatized and laughed at on earth.

My word to you: welcome it.

BIBLICAL EXAMPLES

The Word of God gives us many important examples of men whose primary and only desire was to please God and who lived for an audience of One. Let's take a closer look at some of these men.

Enoch

The first person described by the writer of Hebrews was Enoch. He was commended because he "pleased God" (Heb.

11:5). It does not say he pleased people. It does not say he pleased his family. It does not say he pleased his wife. He pleased God.

Dear reader, do you realize that is the only thing that ultimately matters? We are surrounded by a great cloud of witnesses who lived for one thing: to please God. Our Lord Jesus wants us to be in that vast number—and not be ashamed!

Noah

Noah, "warned by God concerning events as yet *unseen*, in reverent *fear* constructed an ark for the saving of his household" (Heb. 11:7, ESV, emphasis added). He must have felt like an utter fool when building that ark! Imagine people saying to him, "Noah, whatever are you building?" Reply: "An ark." "An ark? Are you serious?" It had never been done before. It was unprecedented. Something yet unseen. That is what makes faith *faith*. He did it for an audience of One.

This is what pleases God. "Without faith it is impossible to please God" (v. 6). Do you want to please God? There is only one way to do it—by faith. Faith plus nothing. Believing God's own Word. I'm sorry, but you can't have it both ways—that is, having the praise of the world and the praise of God. You must make a strategic, deliberate choice: to seek that praise which comes from the only God. The God of the Bible is a jealous God and will not abide competition.

Abraham

By faith alone Abraham was declared righteous (Gen. 15:6). It was also faith alone that led him to offer his son Isaac. It was carried out entirely by obedience to an audience of One. How do you suppose Abraham felt when Isaac said to him, "Where is the lamb for the burnt offering?" Abraham replied, "God himself will provide for himself the lamb for the burnt offering, my son" (Gen. 22:7–8). When Abraham not only became willing but actually began to slaughter Isaac, God stepped in. "Do not lay a hand on the boy....Do not do anything to him. Now I know that you fear God, because you have not withheld from me your son, your only son" (v. 12). And that is when God swore an oath to Abraham (vv. 16–18).

I referred to full assurance earlier in this chapter—when God swears an oath. When this happens, it is the highest level of assurance. It is when God makes Himself *so real* that it is *almost* having no need for mere faith. At least for a while. That is what the oath does. The writer of Hebrews refers to two unchangeable things, namely, the promise and the oath. The oath is stronger. It is "final for confirmation," showing the truth "more convincingly" (Heb. 6:16–18, ESV).

God will not swear an oath to those whose allegiance and need for approval is divided between God and people. It comes to those who are willing to lose everything for Him, an audience of One.

Isaac

Isaac may have been the most lackluster person described in Hebrews 11. But he came through in the end when he affirmed the blessing he gave to Jacob rather than Esau—his firstborn and the son he preferred. He demonstrated in a moment of extreme testing that he loved God more than he did Esau. "Yes, and he [Jacob] shall be blessed" (Gen. 27:33).

Jacob

Jacob did the same thing. When his beloved son Joseph tried to stop his father from giving the greater blessing to Ephraim,

Jacob would not listen to Joseph. Against Joseph's wishes "he put Ephraim ahead of Manasseh" (Gen. 48:20).

Moses

God showed Moses great favor. There was no prophet like him (Deut. 34:10). His ministry became so powerful that the whole of the Old Testament could be summed up in one name: Moses. Indeed the Law came by Moses, grace and truth by Jesus Christ (John 1:17). There was none greater than Moses before Jesus came. So what was Moses' secret? The answer is found when Moses was given the privilege of asking for anything he wanted. In other words, God gave Moses such favor that Moses could "name it and claim it." What was it he wanted? The answer: "If I have found favor in your sight, please show me your ways" (Exod. 33:13, ESV). There you have it. Moses could have asked for *anything*, but he wanted to know God's "ways."

God lamented of ancient Israel, "They have not known my ways" (Heb. 3:10). When Moses could have had anything, he merely wanted to know God's ways. That convicts me and moves me from head to toe.

Joshua

Likewise Joshua, Moses' successor, showed the same reverence to God's ways. When he saw an awesome figure—a man with a drawn sword in his hand—Joshua asked, "Are you for us or for our enemies?" The surprising answer: "Neither...but as commander of the army of the LORD." Instead of objecting or complaining, Joshua fell on his face. He took off his shoes for he was on holy ground (Josh. 5:13–15). This scenario is a perfect demonstration of what I referred to earlier: the only evidence that I have seen the Divine Glory is my willingness to forsake any claim upon God. Joshua saw the Lord's glory. He knew he had no claim upon God. God owed him singularly *nothing*. Joshua accepted this and worshipped.

Samuel

The outstanding thing about Samuel is that he did not take himself seriously or take rejection personally. When Israel demanded a king, Samuel knew it was wrong. But God said to him, "Listen to all that the people are saying to you; it is not you they have rejected, but they have rejected me as their king.... Now listen to them; but warn them solemnly and let them know what the king who will reign over them will claim as his rights" (1 Sam. 8:7, 9). After Samuel warned them sternly and solemnly, the people of Israel said to him, "No...we want a king over us. Then we will be like all the other nations" (vv. 19–20). The Lord then said to Samuel, "Listen to them and give them a king" (v. 22).

The brilliance and humility of Samuel from that moment was that he utterly and totally obeyed the Lord. It would not have mattered to him had people criticized him and said, "How dare you find Israel a king when you yourself said this was so wrong!" But no. By obeying the people, he was literally performing for an audience of One. Samuel worked with all his heart and energy to find them a king. If he were like some of us, he would have said to God, "How can I now find a king for them? I have warned them. My reputation is at stake. Don't make *me* find their king." No. The opposite was true with Samuel. He did not give up until he found Saul son of Kish. Not only that, but he treated Saul as if he were a son— with dignity and honor. You would have thought the whole idea was Samuel's! (See 1 Samuel 9:15–27.) Samuel said to Saul,

"Has not the Lord anointed you to be prince over his people Israel?" (1 Sam. 10:1, esv).

Later on Saul deliberately went against the ceremonial law of Moses when he offered the burnt sacrifice (1 Sam. 13:9). He crossed over a line by putting himself above Scripture. David said to him, "You have done a foolish thing...the Lord has sought out a man after his own heart" (vv. 13–14). From that moment, Saul became yesterday's man, even though he wore the crown for another twenty years. God then told Samuel to go to the house of Jesse and anoint the next king. It is on this occasion we see again how Samuel did not take himself seriously. Once he entered Jesse's house and saw Eliab, Samuel made it obvious that Eliab would be the Lord's anointed. Eliab was the firstborn, and in ancient Israel the firstborn got double the inheritance. But God interrupted and stepped in: "Do not consider his appearance or his height, for I have rejected him. The Lord does not look at the things people look as. People look at the outward appearance, but the Lord looks at the heart" (1 Sam. 16:7). If Samuel took himself seriously and worried about his prophetic reputation, he would have anointed Eliab before Jesse and the sons. But Samuel was not worried about his reputation; he was receiving instructions from an audience of One.

He refused to take rejection personally; he refused to defend his original prophetic impression before this gathering. I'm afraid there are those who won't climb down once they make a statement. They are too proud to admit to a change of mind. That is not all; Samuel did not accept any of the sons Jesse had brought forward. Jesse had not bothered to tell young David to come out and meet the great Samuel. David was tending the sheep. But Samuel felt no need to impress David, nor did he worry about embarrassing Jesse by insisting the next king was not in the room. The man after God's own heart was the young shepherd David—the last man anyone would have predicted to be the next king.

You may feel that you are the most unlikely person to be used in the next move of the Holy Spirit. You may be underestimated because of your age, past, culture, lack of education, or lack of good connections. God knows where you are. He will find you.

David

> The LORD said to Samuel, "How long will you mourn for Saul, since I have rejected him as king over Israel? Fill your horn with oil and be on your way. I am sending you to Jesse of Bethlehem. I have chosen one of his sons to be king."
>
> —1 SAMUEL 16:1

In this verse there is to be found yesterday's man (Saul), today's man (Samuel), and tomorrow's man (David). King Saul wore the crown without the anointing for the next twenty years. David was given the anointing without the crown for another twenty years. David would need those twenty years for preparation. Although the Spirit of God came upon David with power (1 Sam. 16:13), he wasn't truly ready to be king; his anointing would need to be refined. Dr. Martyn Lloyd-Jones used to say to me, "The worst thing that can happen to a man is to succeed before he is ready." God ensured that David would not finish as Saul did—Saul committed suicide (1 Sam. 31:4). David needed those twenty years of preparation; King Saul had none.

All of David's preparation shaped him to reach one goal: to

rule as king before an audience of One. This comes out in the final years of David's kingship—after his grievous sin of adultery and murder. He was chastened severely for his horrible sin, culminating in his son Absalom's taking over the throne.

What reveals David's heart after God was when he was forced into exile. He knew that all that happened was the consequence of his own sin. He did not complain. He never said, "How could this happen to me?" He accepted gracefully the disciplining of his heavenly Father. His finest hour came when his most ardent and faithful supporters were seen carrying the ark of the covenant—to show that God was with David. David might have welcomed this moment. After all the ark was the symbol of God's glory; it represented a prestige and authority that could have caused people to run to David's side. But no. The most moving moment in David's whole life—sometimes it brings me to tears—was when he said to Zadok the priest:

> Take the ark of God back into the city. If I find favor
> in the LORD's eyes, he will bring me back and let me
> see it and his dwelling place again. But if he says, "I am
> not pleased with you," then I am ready; let him do to
> me whatever seems good to him.
> —2 SAMUEL 15:25–26

There you have it—why David was called a man after God's own heart. That is the fruit of one who lives before an audience of One.

Elijah

When the writer of Hebrews referred to women who "received back their dead by resurrection," he was referring to Elijah and Elisha (Heb. 11:35, ESV). When one lives his or her life entirely and exclusively for an audience of One, that person can be trusted to perform the miraculous, including raising the dead. How did Elijah show that he lived for an audience of One? Answer: when he showed fearlessness before King Ahab. First, he said to the king, "As the LORD, the God of Israel, lives, whom I serve, there will be neither dew nor rain in the next few years except at my word" (1 Kings 17:1). Note those words, "before whom I stand" (ESV). His allegiance was to God alone; all he lived for was to listen to and obey God.

Second, he was utterly and completely fearless before Ahab. The king called Elijah "troubler of Israel" (1 Kings 18:17). What an honor to be called that! And yet having such a reputation before royalty and government officials would make most people scared to death. But not Elijah. Partly because of his total devotion and commitment to the God of Israel, Elijah was entrusted not only with a prophetic gift but also the gift of signs and wonders. He raised a widow's son from the dead (1 Kings 17:22–24). He was equally fearless before the prophets of Baal, challenging them before all the people to show that the God of Israel was the true God. The prophets of Baal made fools of themselves trying to get Baal to answer them. When they gave up, Elijah calmly prayed, "Answer me, O LORD, answer me, so these people will know that you, LORD, are God." Then the fire of the Lord fell and the people cried out, "The LORD—he is God! The LORD—he is God!" (1 Kings 18:37–39). God entrusted Elijah with this kind of authority because he was unafraid of what people thought or could do to him.

Elisha

The same was true of his successor, Elisha. He too raised a child from the dead (2 Kings 4:32–37). He also demonstrated a stunning example of applying the principle laid down by Jesus in John 5:44 in a rare way. You may recall that John 5:44 shows why the Jews missed their Messiah. It reads, "How can you believe since you accept glory from one another but do not seek the glory that comes from the only God."

I referred to Elisha earlier. I mention him again because it is an extraordinary example of one who lived for an audience of One. Here is what happened. Elisha healed Naaman the Syrian of leprosy. Naaman, a general and also a very wealthy man, had come in his chariot with the equivalent of millions of dollars today to be healed by Elisha. Naaman was instantly and miraculously healed of his leprosy. He was so grateful. He tried to give Elisha money in order to show his gratitude. But Elisha chose not take any money at all. But right after that his servant Gehazi decided he would exploit the situation and chased Naaman before he left the area in order to tell Naaman a horrible lie—that Elisha changed his mind and would accept a gift after all. Naaman immediately gave Gehazi what he wanted. But when Gehazi returned to Elisha's house, the prophet by revelation saw exactly what Gehazi had done. Elisha pronounced a curse on Gehazi, who became a leper.

But here is the amazing thing: Elisha did not require Gehazi to go back to Naaman and tell him the *truth*, namely, that Gehazi lied and that Elisha in no way wanted a gift. He let Naaman think that he actually asked for the money. Most of us would have wanted to make sure that Naaman knew we were certainly *not* willing to take any money in such a situation. This tells me how utterly committed Elisha was to his audience of One! God knew the truth; that is what mattered to Elisha.

Question: If there were a rumor floating around about you that was absolutely and totally untrue, what would you do? Whether it be something in print or on the internet or word of mouth gossip convincing people right, left, and center, what do you do? Do you defend yourself? Do you persuade a friend to counter the false rumor with your version of the truth?

It must have given Elisha enormous satisfaction to refuse money from Naaman the Syrian general. It was a testimony to the God of Israel. It demonstrated that God is gracious and that His power is not for sale. What is more, Naaman must have admired Elisha no end. Elisha would have known this. But now Gehazi has gotten money from Naaman, who can no longer have quite the same admiration toward Elisha. This surely would have dampened Elisha's spirit. It would have hurt a lot. But Elisha did nothing. He did not make Gehazi tell the truth to Naaman. Why? Because God knew the *truth* and the *truth* mattered more to Elisha than clearing his name.

Question: Would Elisha have been in the wrong to instruct Gehazi to tell Naaman the truth? Probably not. But it does show a rather unusual degree of grace not to worry over what people think—especially if it is a case of people who have admired you but they may start admiring you less. It was as though Elisha had been guided by wisdom like that of Paul centuries later: to wait until God steps in to reveal the truth—"At that time each will receive their praise from God" (1 Cor. 4:5).

The question is: Can you and I wait that long?

Shadrach, Meshach, and Abednego

I have three grandsons—Tobias (Toby), Timothy, and Tyndale (Ty). I pray daily for them that they will be like Shadrach, Meshach, and Abednego, those stalwart Hebrew heroes who were banished from Jerusalem during the days of the Babylonian captivity. They are referred to in Hebrews 11:34 as those who "quenched the fury of the flames." It happened when King Nebuchadnezzar demanded that all the people bow down to the image he had made. Those who refused would be thrown into a burning fiery furnace. As soon as the music began, every single person was required to bow down. But these three men refused. This made the king angry. They were brought before the king. The king asked them, "What god will be able to rescue you from my hand?" Their reply: "King Nebuchadnezzar, we do not need to defend ourselves before you in this matter. If we are thrown into the blazing furnace, the God we serve is able to deliver us from it, and he will deliver us from Your Majesty's hand. But even if he does not, we want you to know, Your Majesty, that we will not serve your gods or worship the image of gold you have set up" (Dan. 3:16–18).

Question: Do you have the "but if not" faith? That is what motivated these three Hebrews. They knew that God could deliver them, "but if not"—even if He didn't—they would not bow down. They were governed by an audience of One.

They were immediately thrown into the burning fiery furnace. But the only thing that was burnt was the rope that had been tied to their hands when they were thrown into the fire. Not only were the three men unhurt but with them was a *fourth man*—"like a son of the gods" (v. 25). This may be seen as someone—a type of Christ—who not only joined Shadrach, Meshach, and Abednego but quenched the power of fire. This also demonstrates a most important truth: God does not promise to take us out of the fire, but He promises to get into the fire with us.

Daniel

Daniel, like Samuel, is a canonical prophet—that is, unlike Elijah and Elisha, he has a book of the Bible named after him. The phrase "shut the mouths of lions" (Heb. 11:33) refers to

Daniel. The evidence that Daniel lived for an audience of One is when he "went home to his upstairs room where the windows opened toward Jerusalem" (Dan. 6:10).

Here is the background. Daniel had been given a promotion in the royal court; he "so distinguished himself" above all the others (v. 3). The reason: there was "an excellent spirit in him" (ESV). This made people jealous of Daniel. The king planned to set him over the entire kingdom. Daniel's enemies sought to find ground for complaint against him, "but they could find no ground for complaint...because he was faithful, and no error or fault was found in him" (v. 4, ESV). Then these men concluded, "We shall not find any ground for complaint against this Daniel unless we find it in connection with the law of his God" (v. 5, ESV).

It is a wonderful testimony of your faith if your enemies cannot find fault in you unless it has to do with your relationship with God! So it was with Daniel. The enemies appealed to the king to sign a decree that "cannot be changed" (v. 8, ESV) whereby no one could petition "any god or man" except "to you, O king" (v. 7, ESV). Those who did not honor this decree would be "cast into the den of lions" (v. 7, ESV).

What did Daniel do? I suspect that many of us what find it providential that we don't have to take such a strong stand for our convictions. After all the king signed a decree. It was now law. We might tell ourselves that surely God does not want us to stir up trouble for ourselves or lose our lives for a small thing such as praying. Or, if we insist on praying, we could do it so that nobody would find out. So what did Daniel do?

> When Daniel knew that the document had been signed, he went to his house where he had windows in his upper chamber open toward Jerusalem. He got

down on his knees three times a day and prayed and
gave thanks before his God, as he had done previously.

—DANIEL 6:10, ESV

The result was that Daniel was thrown into the lions' den.
It happened that the king had great respect for Daniel and
knew that he had been tricked by jealous people in his court.
But even the king himself could not change the decree he had
signed. After Daniel was thrown into the den of lions, the king
spent a sleepless night. At the break of day he rushed to the
den to inquire whether Daniel's God had preserved him. Daniel
was alive and well! He answered the king: "My God sent his
angel, and he shut the mouths of the lions" (v. 22). After that
the accusers of Daniel were thrown into the lions' den and were
immediately devoured by the hungry lions (v. 24).

Others: "of whom the world was not worthy"

I do need to add an important PS to this chapter. Since I
have selected certain people from Hebrews 11 who chose to
live before an audience of One, it must be observed that not
all those people who lived for audience of One by faith had the
same happy outcome. There is a very important word toward
the end this chapter: "others."

Others suffered mocking and flogging, and even
chains and imprisonment. They were stoned, they
were sawn in two, they were killed with the sword.
They went about in skins of sheep and goats, desti-
tute, afflicted, mistreated—of whom the world was not
worthy—wandering about in deserts and mountains,
and in dens and caves of the earth.

—HEBREWS 11:36–38, ESV

I feel I must add at least two men in New Testament times that deserve a place in the Faith Hall of Fame. Both are examples of great grace.

The apostle Peter

Here is a man who denied knowing Jesus after having walked with Jesus, been spoon-fed by Jesus, and been loved by Jesus for three years (Matt. 26:69–75). Having done that, Peter was *so sorry, so ashamed.* But there was a positive benefit: he not only learned his lesson, but it pretty much eradicated any self-righteousness in him. That is one of the reasons God could use Peter on the day of Pentecost.

I remember sitting beside the pulpit one Sunday morning at Westminster Chapel. I bowed my head just before the doxology was sung. I was devastated. I had spoken crossly to Louise just before I left our apartment and walked to the chapel. I so wanted to apologize, but it was too late to go back home. As I prayed, I said, "Lord, however can You use me today? I am so in the wrong, so utterly unqualified to be here and so ashamed. Please forgive me." Guess what? I preached that day with more power than I had known in a long time. I am totally convinced the reason was that I was devoid of self-righteousness. I believe my feeling of worthlessness was the reason God could use me.

These things said, God used Peter mightily for years, as seen in the Book of Acts.

He lived for an audience of One for the rest of his days. A good example is when he obeyed a strange vision—seeing, "something like a large sheet being let down to earth by its four corners. It contained all kinds of four-footed animals, as well as reptiles and birds. Then a voice told him, 'Get up, Peter. Kill and eat.' 'Surely not, Lord!'...'I have never eaten anything impure or unclean.' The voice spoke to him a second time, 'Do not call anything impure that God has made clean'" (Acts 10:11–15). Peter obeyed, going right against his legalistic tradition that upheld the Levitical Law.

That was huge for Peter. Not only that, but his obedience paved the way for him to go against another tradition and associate with Gentiles (vv. 28–29). It was a pivotal point in the history of Christianity. Knowing that this could make him unpopular with Jews—including Jewish believers—Peter chose to obey an audience of One. Later on, when Jewish believers accused him of fraternizing with Gentiles, Peter did not scold them. He did not say, "How dare you talk to me like that! I am the Lord's apostle!" No. Speaking before an audience of One, he patiently explained to his fellow Jews how God had brought him to this change of view in his life (Acts 11:2–17). He did this so well that these Jewish believers climbed down from their bias and actually glorified God, saying, "Then, even to Gentiles God has granted repentance that leads to life" (v. 18).

The apostle Paul

Paul too was a trophy of great grace. He never forgot how unworthy he was to be saved. He was possibly the greatest persecutor of the church that ever was. He also may have had the most extraordinary conversion that ever was! God miraculously saved him, but it was also shown that he would suffer (Acts 9:16). He was even called to be an apostle.

The first person (that I know of) to be converted under my ministry at Westminster Chapel was Jay Michaels, a Los Angeles Jew and businessman. His secretary in London invited him to a Sunday night service at the chapel. He was converted the same night, but I did not hear about it for a good while. That said, we became very good friends; I took him fishing in the Florida Keys. He said to me one day, "Before I became a

Christian, I was a happy man." Those were his exact words. He wasn't complaining. He was only pointing out that things had not gone so well for him since he was saved. His wife and family were not open to the gospel. It was not easy for him.

This brings up the question: Why be a Christian? Is it because it will make you happier? Maybe yes, maybe no. Will it help your marriage? Maybe yes, maybe no. Why be a Christian? The main and primary answer is found when you discover why Jesus died on the cross. The most popular verse in the Bible is John 3:16—the Bible in a nutshell—"For God so loved the world that he gave his one and only Son, that whoever believes in him shall not perish but have eternal life." Note the phrase *shall not perish*. This is a reference to eternal punishment in hell. That is why Jesus died.

Suppose we ask Paul to testify regarding "what being a Christian has meant to me." What do you suppose he would say? Try this for his testimony—his very words that show what life was like for Paul since he was saved:

> Five times I received from the Jews the forty lashes minus one. Three times I was beaten with rods, once I was pelted with stones, three times I was shipwrecked, I spent a night and a day in the open sea, I have been constantly on the move. I have been in danger from rivers, in danger from bandits, in danger from my fellow Jews, in danger from Gentiles; in danger in the city, in danger in the country, in danger at sea; and in danger from false believers. I have labored and toiled and have often gone without sleep; I have known hunger and thirst and have often gone without food; I have been cold and naked.
>
> —2 CORINTHIANS 11:24–27

What kept Paul going? He lived for an audience of One. His supreme ambition: "I want to know Christ—yes, to know the power of his resurrection and participation in his sufferings, becoming like him in his death" (Phil. 3:10). This verse explains the apostle Paul.

Caution: never—ever—presume that your faithfulness to God by being devoted to an audience of One is a guarantee of blessing, prosperity, health, happiness, and safety. "The blood of the martyrs is the seed of the church," said Tertullian (155–220).[2] By this he meant that God uses the death and suffering of His saints to cause the church to grow all the more. And yet this is not always true either! Sometimes it would seem Satan has a temporary victory. In any case, you and I must not live before an audience of One because it will guarantee blessing. But I can, however, tell you what it will guarantee: a reward at the judgment seat of Christ.

Chapter Nine

A SPARK

—————— ◆◆ ——————

Consider what a great forest is set on fire by a small spark.
—**James 3:5**

Adairville was where the spark came that ignited
the Second Great Awakening. The first camp
meeting began at Red River Church House.
—**Ricky Skaggs**

I F A WOMAN begins shouting in the middle of taking the Lord's Supper, should she be stopped? Or encouraged?

That is a question a guest preacher was wrestling with when he was in charge of the Lord's Supper at the Red River Meeting House in Logan County, Kentucky, in June 1800.

What happened was this. A woman began shouting spontaneously and loudly during the sacrament of the Lord's Supper at a service. This led eventually to the Cane Ridge Revival of 1801. That a woman *shouting* led in some way to the Cane Ridge phenomenon is a historical fact and not under dispute. What could be debated is whether her shouting and what followed afterward was the work of the Holy Spirit, the flesh, or the devil.

I have referred to the Cane Ridge Revival of 1801 in several of my books, the first of these being in *Stand Up and Be Counted*. That small book offers a biblical rationale for giving an invitation for people to confess Christ publicly after preaching the gospel. Billy Graham kindly wrote a brief foreword to it. I have since sought to learn all I could about the Cane Ridge Revival, known as America's Second Great Awakening, the first being the New England Great Awakening that took place mostly in Massachusetts and Connecticut in approximately 1720–1760.

I happened to tell Ricky Skaggs that I was preaching in a Baptist church in Adairville, Kentucky. He wrote back immediately and made the statement quoted at the beginning of the chapter regarding "the spark" that ignited the fire that led to America's Second Great Awakening. I had forgotten that this small town in Logan County is very near where the old Red River Meeting House was located—a spot of vital importance in American church history. When I arrived at this church, I inquired if there might be anyone around who could tell me more about what happened there almost two hundred years ago?

There was. A couple whose property is adjacent to the Red River Meeting House shared a lot of valuable material with me. They had dozens of articles and letters written by eyewitnesses of what happened in 1800—a year *prior* to the Cane Ridge Revival of 1801. The more I read of what they kindly gave me, the more I was gripped. I began to see that what I learned from these papers warranted a chapter in this book. What I discovered is not new to the scholars who have written on this era of American church history. But much I learned was fresh to me. Sadly there are no dates or names on many of the documents, but copies are in my files and the documents appear authentic to me. It should be noted that some of the people quoted in this chapter were not skillful or educated writers, neither did they always say things as clearly as we would wish.

Because the Red River Meeting House is in Logan County and Cane Ridge is in Bourbon County—both being in Kentucky—some hastily assume the two outpourings of the Holy Spirit are one and the same. Whereas the two phenomena are organically connected, they were a year apart, and a Logan County is approximately two hundred miles west southwest of Bourbon County, where Cane Ridge is located. Cane Ridge was where America's Second Great Awakening eventually took place a year later in August 1801.

Earlier in this book I referred to the spark that could ignite a forest fire by lack of controlling the tongue. But in this chapter I want to suggest that a spark from the tongue—out of obedience to the audience of One—can be a good thing!

It is what happened in the summer of 1800 in Logan County

that equally fascinates me—the spark that ignited in the old Red River Meeting House.

JAMES MCGREADY (1763–1817)

One of the important figures that eventually led to the Cane Ridge Revival of 1800 was James McGready, a thirty-three year old Presbyterian who moved from North Carolina to Logan County, Kentucky, in 1796. It was his ministry that paved the way for what would happen in June 1800. He had been rejected by his church in North Carolina for preaching what was called "revival doctrine." In a word, he talked about the witness of the Holy Spirit consciously assuring a person that he or she was truly born again. This was perceived by many of his hearers as new teaching—if not heretical and it did not sit well with many Calvinists who assumed that their moral living proved they were truly converted and therefore among God's elect. McGready never wavered on his Calvinism, believing in divine election but stressing that people should have intimacy with God—sometimes called *experimental religion*. He became the pastor of three churches simultaneously in Logan County—one at Red River, one at Muddy River near Russellville, the other by Gasper River. The entire membership of the three churches consisted of less than a hundred people, with two or three dozen in each of these small meeting houses. There was constant opposition to his preaching in these places of worship.

McGready spoke, lived, and preached before an audience of One. He learned to be unafraid of man and listened to God. One who knew him said of him:

> Like Enoch, he walked with God; like Jacob, he wres-
> tled with God...like Elijah, he was very jealous for the

Lord God of hosts....He was remarkably plain in his dress and manners....He possessed a sound understanding, and a moderate share of human learning. The style of his sermons was not polished, but perspicuous and pointed; and his manner [of] address was unusually solemn and impressive....He was hated, and sometimes bitterly reproached and persecuted, not only by the openly vicious and profane, but by many nominal Christians, or formal professors, who could not bear heart-searching and penetrating addresses, and the indignation of the Almighty against the ungodly, which, as a son of thunder, he clearly presented to the view of their guilty minds from the awful denunciations of the Word of Truth. Although he did not fail to preach Jesus Christ, and him crucified...he was more distinguished by a talent for depicting the guilty and deplorable situation of impenitent sinners, and the awful consequences of their rebellion against God, without speedy repentance unto life, and a living faith in the blood of sprinkling.[1]

You must keep in mind that McGready had not been trained in "seeker friendly" type of ministry. The preaching of hell-fire and damnation was an assumption that lay behind all he taught. He did not think twice about it. It was said that McGready "could almost make you feel that the dreadful abyss of perdition lay yawning beneath you, and you could almost hear the wails of the lost and see them writhing as they floated on the lurid billows of that hot sea of flame in the world of woe." One person remarked that his voice "was like a trumpet; you could hear it with ease several hundred [yards away]."[2]

What happened in June 1800 was the culmination of McGready's preaching for the previous four years in Logan

County. There were tokens of revival during those years, with a number of people being converted at Red River and also in the Muddy River and Gasper River meeting houses. There were other ministers involved as well at various times during these years, so one must not give and undue amount of credit to McGready alone. In fact McGready was not the preacher in the pulpit when the spark ignited, as we will see below. But a great sense of the presence of the Holy Spirit was felt in all three of his congregations in the years leading up to June 1800.

McGready placed a strong emphasis on the Lord's Supper. He managed to get a number of the people to sign a covenant. He presented to the members of his congregations for their approval and signatures a covenant that included these words; to this they affixed their names:

> We feel encouraged to unite our supplications to a prayer hearing God, for the outpouring of his spirit, that his people may be quickened and comforted, and that our children, and sinners generally, may be converted. Therefore, we bind ourselves to observe the third Saturday of each month, for one year, as a day of fasting and prayer, for the conversion of sinners in Logan county, and throughout the world. We also engage to spend one half hour every Saturday evening, beginning at the setting of the sun, and one half hour ever Sabbath morning, at the rising of the sun, in pleading with God to revive his work.[3]

THE SPARK

"The year 1800 exceeds all that my eyes ever beheld upon earth," wrote McGready in a letter to a friend.[4] McGready planned to have different ministers to speak in services on a Sunday, Monday, and Tuesday in June 1800. It was agreed that the sacrament of the Lord's Supper be carried out on the Monday. "This was the greatest time we had ever seen before. On Monday multitudes were struck down under awful conviction."[5] On the previous Sunday a number of Presbyterian ministers plus a Methodist minister participated in the services. A sense of the presence of God reportedly set in. The services that Sunday were said to be "animated, and tears flowed freely."[6]

But nothing extraordinary was noticed until Monday—during the sacrament—when a visiting Presbyterian minister named William Hodge (c. 1747–c. 1819) from Sumner County, Tennessee, was preaching and conducting the sacrament of the Lord's Supper. One reported:

> Many had such clear and heart piercing views of their sinfulness, and the danger to which they were exposed, that they fell prostrate on the floor, and their cries filled the house....Those who had been the most outbreaking sinners, were to be seen laying on the floor unable to help themselves, and anxiously enquiring what they should do to be saved....Persons of all classes, and of all ages were to be seen in agonies, and heard crying for redemption in the blood of [the] Lamb.[7]

Strange as it may seem, by all accounts this outpouring of the Spirit began with a woman shouting loudly and spontaneously during the service centered on the Lord's Supper. All the documents I have found regarding the Monday service at the Red River Meeting House state what follows or coheres with this account:

A woman in the extreme end of the house, unable
to control the violence of her emotions, gave vent to
them in loud cries.[8]

Another witness reported it this way:

A woman in the east end of the house got an uncommon
blessing, broke through order, and shouted for some
time, and then sat down in silence.[9]

The same account simply states:

A woman in the east end of the house shouted
tremendously.[10]

There is a consensus that "this was the beginning of that glorious revival of religion in this Country, which was so great a
blessing to thousands; and from this meeting Camp-meetings
took their rise."[11]

There was to be an intermission after the Lord's Supper,
but the people did not leave their seats. Instead they "wept
in silence all over the house."[12] An acute sense of the Holy
Spirit's presence reportedly settled on the people. An eye-
witness named John McGee described his experience in this
service, stating that the guest preacher William Hodge, "felt
such a power come on him, that he quit his seat, and sat down
in the floor of the pulpit, (I suppose not knowing what he did)."
McGee said that "a power which caused me to tremble, was
upon me." He added:

There was a solemn weeping all over the house. Having
a wish to preach, I strove against my feelings; at length
I rose up and told the people, I was appointed to
preach, but there was a greater than I preaching, and

exhorted them to let the Lord God Omnipotent reign in their hearts, and to submit to Him, and their souls should live.[13]

Keep in mind that McGee was a visiting preacher, not the pastor, although the pastor, McGready, was in the congregation. McGee described what happened next:

> I left the pulpit to go to [the woman shouting], and as I went along through the people, it was suggested to me, "You know these people [being Presbyterians] are much for order, they will not bear this confusion, go back and be quiet." I turned to go back, and was near falling; the power of God was strong upon me, I turned again, and loosing sight of the fear of man, I went through the house shouting, and exhorting with all possible ecstasy and energy, and the floor was soon covered with the slain; their screams for mercy pierced the heavens, and mercy came down; some found forgiveness, and many went away from that meeting, feeling unutterable agonies of soul for redemption in the blood of Jesus.[14]

In a word, the woman shouting was the spark.

SOME OBSERVATIONS

When the preacher "left the pulpit to go to her," it was possibly to quiet her. Some report that it was to comfort her. It is not clear whether the suggestion was in McGee's own mind—from what he called "the fear of man"—or if someone was audibly cautioning him. All we know is that he said, "I turned to go back." That apparently meant he changed his mind that he approach the woman. Therefore, after making a few steps toward the woman, he made the decision to go back to the pulpit and sit down. This could have been the crucial, if not the pivotal, moment. He obviously changed his mind about going up to her. To comfort her would have ensured that the work of the Spirit would not be quenched. To quiet her would have been a "Presbyterian" thing to do, to say, "Calm down, sister." Or quietly escort her out of the meeting house.

But he did not go to her; he did not stop her.

The suggestion, "These people are much for order, they will not bear this confusion," was probably in his own mind—that he feared what all the people might be thinking when this woman shouted and kept shouting. It was the fear of man that put this suggestion in his mind. Even if someone audibly made the suggestion to him, he rejected it. He may have felt he should comfort her; he may have felt he should quiet her to show he wanted order and therefore leave no room for allowing confusion. In any case, he says that he overcame fear. Perhaps he had wondered what McGready might be thinking. We will see below that McGready was somewhat nervous about what happened.

In a word, a guest preacher was an unsung hero of what became the Cane Ridge Revival a year later. He deliberately decided *not* to approach the woman but then got over what anyone might think and began exhorting as he did. I would add it was the Holy Spirit on him that emancipated him from the fear of the people. One can be sure that McGee exhorting as he did affirmed and comforted the woman who did the shouting.

What we know is that—thankfully—no one stopped the outburst, *the spark*. McGee instead proceeded to exhort the people. The result was that many men and women, "over-whelmed with conviction, fell to the floor and would remain prostrate and motionless for hours, but when they arose with the shout of victory, they would testify that they were conscious through the experience."[15] In other words, though on the floor motionless, they were fully aware of what was going on.

After the Red River service McGready was said to be surprised and astonished at the apparent confusion in the meeting house. He asked, "What is to be done?" An elder, "looking in at the door, and seeing all on the floor, praising or praying, said, 'We can do nothing. If this be of Satan, it will soon come to an end; but if it is of God, our efforts and fears are in vain. I think it is of God, and will join in ascribing glory to His name.'" Those who arose from the floor were reportedly "shouting praise, for the evidences felt in their own souls, of sins forgiven—for 'redeeming grace and dying love.'"[16]

It was further reported that "there remained no more place that day, for preaching or administering the Supper."[17] I assume this meant no place for *continuing* to administer the Supper since it seems to have begun. But after the woman shouted and the people began to scream and fall to the floor, apparently Hodge did not preach his prepared sermon, nor did they finish administering the Supper. The people were so much under the influence of the conscious presence of the Holy Spirit that they did not move. Around forty-five people professed to be converted that evening.

Such was the result of the spark that caused a historic fire in Logan County.

We have observed that McGready was not in charge of this service. He possibly would have known the woman—whether she was an upstanding woman of God or an unstable person with emotional problems. To comment on what McGready might have done had he been leading the service would be unprofitable speculation. What we know is that a guest preacher was in charge.

We cannot enter the woman's mind—whether she was worshipping in ecstasy or feared for her own soul. Either way it was, in my view, God's conscious presence that precipitated her shouting. The Cane Ridge Revival that followed in 1801 is good evidence of that.

One more comment: it is my opinion that McGee would almost certainly have put out the Spirit's fire had he reached the woman and calmed her down. The apostle Paul's word, "Quench not the Spirit" (1 Thess. 5:19, KJV), is relevant here. Had McGee stopped her shouting in front of all present, the atmosphere would have changed abruptly. The weeping would probably have stopped. There probably would have been no people prostrate and motionless on the floor. We would therefore never have heard of the Red River Meeting House. And there would have been no Cane Ridge Revival a year later.

But thanks to McGee's turning back from approaching the woman, the Spirit was not quenched.

When we get to heaven, we can watch a video replay of the whole scenario.

As a consequence of the Monday service at Red River, this same sense of the presence of God spread to McGready's two other congregations. During June, July, and August of 1800 the people from all three congregations witnessed the same phenomena. It was always entirely spontaneous. Nobody had prayed for this woman to shout as she did. No one expected this. For all I know, nobody wanted it. But once the woman shouted—and was not stopped—the people began to fall. The exact same thing thus continued all summer in the three meeting houses in Logan County. People came in covered wagons to camp and to see what was going on.

Whereas the "falling exercise[s]"[18] that prevailed so extensively in McGready's three congregations were unprecedented in Logan County, they were not without precedent elsewhere. The same kind of falling was referred to as "swooning" during the New England Awakening. Jonathan Edwards' wife was in such a state for several days. She said she was overwhelmed from experiencing the sense of "his nearness to me, and of my dearness to him."[19]

These falling exercises reappeared the following summer in Cane Ridge, as we will see below.

THE HORRIBLE FEAR OF BEING LOST

When we who live in Britain or America in the twenty-first century read about these revivals of over two hundred years ago, it is hard to get into the skin of the people who were so emotional. It is natural for us to dismiss it all as irrelevant for our day since these people were uncultured, uneducated, and unsophisticated. There is certainly truth to this. But there is another factor we might not have thought about. The preaching of eternal damnation was common but generally made no impact at all until the revival came. The assumption in all that McGready taught and preached was that if you were not converted—and did not know you were born again by the witness of the Spirit—you would go to hell forever. And yet this preaching alone made little or no impact on society. The frontiersmen in those days who did not go to church were known for their disregard for the church or anything sacred and for their wickedness, debauchery, and dishonesty. Not only that, the influence of Thomas Paine, to be examined below, had left many people with the feeling that there was nothing to worry about since the Bible was not true and there was consequently no heaven, no hell, no God. That assumption had spread to the grassroots.

It was the Holy Spirit sovereignly stepping in that changed all this. The famous meeting in Red River, and its spreading to the other congregations, came after three to four years of praying and fasting by the faithful few. Therefore, when the Spirit of God came down, men and women were literally shaken rigid. The fear of being lost—or not being chosen—did not bother people in the world who were uninfluenced by the Spirit. But when the Holy Spirit set in, everything changed. So much so that men actually came to the services to scoff but were themselves stricken by the Spirit and laid flat out on the ground.

It must be realized, therefore, that both in Red River and in Cane Ridge the fear of being eternally lost—or in some cases the fear of not being one of God's elect—surfaced only when the Holy Spirit came in power. This is was what lay behind the groans and their falling down helplessly. They suddenly feared for their own eternal destiny. For that reason the Spirit's witness that they were saved and not eternally lost gave them ecstatic joy that caused the noise that could be heard. The most important factor was the issue of assurance of salvation. In some cases there were two stages of emotional outburst:

1. The groans that came from the fear of being lost.

2. The overwhelming sense of relief that finally
   came that one was not going to hell but was
   saved.

The latter was the main thing that caused the loud shouting. The relief, assurance, and joy that people received led them to yell at the top of their voices.

This was thus the beginning of camp meetings. People traveled from Sumner County in Tennessee, probably following Hodge, to Logan County, Kentucky. There was only one covered wagon present at the meeting at Red River, but more wagons came to Muddy River. This practice of people coming in covered wagons to camp and stay around rapidly increased from then on.

THE AGE OF REASON

Prior to the movement of the Holy Spirit in Kentucky in the late eighteenth century was a fast growing sense of unbelief in the Bible. What McGready and his fellow Presbyterians fought against was not only skepticism among believers but an ever-increasing atheism in society generally.

Thomas Paine (1737–1809) was born in England. His book *The Age of Reason*, written largely through the influence of the French philosopher Voltaire (1694–1778), became widely read. He came to the British American colonies in 1774. He espoused the position of the colonists in the American Revolution. This gave him considerable acceptance. Paine had learned through his time in France that the French people had strongly rejected religion and sacred things. He then wrote *The Age of Reason* against the Bible as being the Word of God. It became a popular book and had an extensive circulation, including in

Kentucky. As a result the Bible found a place only in religious families. It was estimated that among "intelligent" people who called themselves Christian toward the close of the eighteenth century, the majority of the population were either professed infidels or skeptically inclined. For example, there were few in the professions of law and science who would avow their belief in the truth of Christianity.

It was during this religious dearth that the revival had its origins in Logan County, Kentucky, as well as in Bourbon County, Kentucky. The ministries of men like James McGready had to overcome the prejudices of many people who had succumbed to the influence of Thomas Paine.

It may be wondered, "How there could have been a Bible belt throughout the South in the past several generations?" It was therefore not reason or logic but the power of the Holy Spirit that overcame much of Paine's influence. Barton Stone (1772–1844), referred to later in this chapter, would later observe, "The effects of this meeting [referring to the Cane Ridge Revival] through the country were like fire in dry stubble driven by a strong wind."[20] It was concluded by J. M. Peck in *The Christian Review* (1852): "Infidelity received its death blow during that revival period."[21]

THE CANE RIDGE REVIVAL OF 1801

Rev. Barton Stone, a convert of McGready from several years back, became the pastor of a Presbyterian church in Cane Ridge in Bourbon County, Kentucky. Hearing of what was going on among McGready's three congregations, he traveled to Logan County in the summer of 1800 in to investigate. Stone wrote:

The scene to me was new, and passing strange. It baffled description. Many, very many fell down, as men slain in battle, and continued for hours together in an apparently breathless and motionless state....After lying thus for hours, they obtained deliverance.... With astonishment did I hear men, women and children declaring the wonderful works of God, and the glorious mysteries of the gospel. Their appeals were solemn, heart-penetrating, bold and free. Under such [preaching] many others would fall down into the same state....

My conviction was complete that it was a good work—the work of God; nor has my mind wavered since on the subject. Much did I then see, and much have I since seen, that I considered to be fanaticism; but this should not condemn the work. The Devil has always tried to ape the works of God, to bring them into disrepute. But that cannot be a Satanic work, which brings men to humble confession and forsaking of sin—to solemn prayer—fervent praise and thanksgiving, and to sincere and affectionate exhortations to sinners to repent and go to Jesus the Saviour.[22]

While present in Logan County, Stone noticed many covered wagons that carried people from various places to observe these unusual phenomena. He suggested that people meet the following year at Cane Ridge, this being a more suitable place for camp meetings. Word spread quickly. The following summer thousands came in their covered wagons from near and far to meet for fellowship and Bible study. This took place in August 1801. Crowds were estimated from ten to twenty thousand; one observer even estimated thirty thousand.

A general camp meeting began at Cane Ridge on August 6, 1801. That is when people began to arrive in their covered wagons. On the Sunday morning, August 9, a Methodist minister, William Burke—some sources state that he was a lay minister—arrived, apparently expecting to speak, but he received no invitation from the Presbyterians in charge to preach or have any part in the services. Sometime after ten o'clock that morning he found "a convenient place on the body of a fallen tree." Some reports state that the fallen tree was about fifteen feet above the ground. He began "reading a hymn with an audible voice," and, Burke reported, "by the time we concluded singing and praying, we had around us, standing on their feet, by fair calculation, ten thousand people. I gave out my text in the following words: 'For we shall all stand before the judgment-seat of Christ' [2 Cor. 5:10]." Burke stated that "before I concluded, my voice was not to be heard for the groans of distress and the shouts of triumph."[23] Burke described what he witnessed:

> Hundreds fell prostrate to the ground, and work [of the Holy Spirit] continued on that spot till Wednesday afternoon. It was estimated by some that not less than five hundred were at one time lying on the ground in the deepest agonies of distress, and every few minutes rising in shouts of triumph.... I remained Sunday and Sunday night, and Monday and Monday night; and during that time there was not a single moment's cessation, but the work went on, and old and young, men, women, and children, were converted to God. It was estimated that on Sunday and Sunday night there were twenty thousand people on the ground.[24]

This phenomenon continued through Wednesday, during which time there were reportedly no fewer than five hundred on the ground at any moment. At first it was feared that these people were dead. Panic set in with some. They had trouble finding a pulse. Sometimes only two beats a minute. But after a few hours, without exception, these people got up and shouted at the top of their voices with joy and assurance that they were truly saved. It has since been called America's Second Great Awakening. The "roar of Niagara"[25] came to mind as people could hear the shouts of men and women and children from nearly a mile away. Whereas the Great Awakening in New England lasted for fifteen years or more, the Cane Ridge Revival lasted approximately four days—mainly from Sunday through Wednesday. It shows how much God can accomplish in a very short period of time. On Thursday people began returning to their homes, having to get to their jobs. Stone wrote, "A particular description of this meeting would fill a large volume, and then half would not be told."[26]

SOME CONCLUDING OBSERVATIONS

The spark referred to in James 3:5 had to do with controlling the tongue. The slightest unguarded comment could be a spark that set a forest on fire.

The spark that ignited the revival in Logan County, Kentucky—leading to the Cane Ridge Revival—could have been extinguished. It is impossible to know whether the preacher William Hodge initially intended to shut up the woman who started shouting or if he was going to comfort her. In either case, he did not approach her but turned back and let her continue. And the rest is history.

I have wondered what kind of vulnerability it might take that you and I would be a spark today. Are we so orderly and sophisticated that our usual way of doing things will put out the Spirit's fire?

Would you be vulnerable? Would I?

I suspect if a woman shouted in the middle of the Lord's Supper today, in any church, she would be immediately silenced. I also fear that if I myself were conducting the Lord's Supper and this happened, I would be very suspicious, very uneasy, and very keen to have her stopped. On the other hand, if I had a great sense of the conscious presence of God when this happened, I'd like to think I would not interrupt it. It is very hard to imagine what it was really like in those days.

In the years that followed the Cane Ridge Revival, there emerged diverse opinions theologically. First, not all those involved in the Cane Ridge Revival were Calvinists. Many Methodists joined with the Presbyterians in this meeting. As we saw, Burke was a Methodist. There were a few Baptists. There were also some ministers both in Logan County and Bourbon County churches that reportedly abandoned their Calvinism. This included Barton Stone, who eventually left the Presbyterian church. He became a founder of the Christian Church, also known as the Disciples of Christ. Whereas James McGready never wavered in his theology, he never made much of his belief regarding election and predestination. Second, there was a division in the aftermath of Cane Ridge as to whether a minister needed to be educated. Presbyterians were strong on this point—that a minister should be well educated before being ordained. But because of the spontaneity and enablement that characterized much of the preaching that came out of the Cane Ridge Revival, many felt it was quite *wrong* for a preacher to be educated.

I myself grew up in Ashland, Kentucky, some one hundred miles from Cane Ridge. The effect of the Cane Ridge Revival went all over Kentucky and into neighboring states. There was still a widespread feeling in my area that preachers did not need to be formally educated. I was influenced by many un-educated evangelists and pastors. None of them (as far as I know) had university degrees. Some of these men helped to shape my thinking as I grew up.

There is a striking similarity between the preaching con-tent in the first Great Awakening and the preaching content in the Second Great Awakening: both dealt with the future judgment and people's final destiny. First, you may recall that McGready's preaching in Logan County was described as having an emphasis on hell. God eventually honored this with the spark that ignited the fire that led to the Cane Ridge Revival. Second, Jonathan Edwards' sermon "Sinners in the Hands of an Angry God"—preached July 8, 1741, in Enfield, Connecticut—was about eternal punishment in hell. God honored this with such conviction that people held on to church pews and tree trunks to keep from sliding into hell. The world never forgot it. When people think of the New England Awakening, they often think of Edwards' sermon immediately. Third, William Burke took his text in Cane Ridge from 2 Corinthians 5:10: "We must all appear before the judgment seat of Christ." God honored Burke's preaching by thousands being convicted and falling helplessly to the ground—as "men slain in battle," observed Barton Stone. This is largely what is remembered when people think of the Cane Ridge Revival.

There was another strange phenomenon that came from

Cane Ridge: a certain style of preaching. What I did not report previously was that there were at times at least five different men preaching simultaneously among the crowds of thousands at Cane Ridge. Some report that there were seven different men preaching—some from tree stumps, some from covered wagons. I am not able to describe this style in writing. These men were not preaching from prepared manuscripts. The best I can do is to say that many preachers in those days not only shouted loudly but needed to take a deep breath between nearly every word or two as they exhorted! It was as though they were gasping for breath as they preached. I honestly suspect that at first this *could* have been a result of the Spirit's power—the *kabod* (Hebrew word for *heaviness* but often translated "glory") on them. But after the revival subsided there were those who needed to keep this up—to prove that they still had the anointing. Or to have the "hoyle" (*hwyl*), as they would say in Wales!

THE TORONTO BLESSING AND CANE RIDGE

One further observation. One of the earmarks of the Toronto Blessing that emerged in 1994 was the falling, often accompanied with *laughter.* Joy. This also happened in the Cane Ridge Revival. There were at least three differences. First, the audible groanings and the ecstasy at Red River and Cane Ridge came in the context of the preaching of eternal judgment. When the Holy Spirit endorsed the preaching of people like James McGready the Presbyterian and William Burke the Methodist, the people were suddenly seized with conviction of sin and fear of being hopelessly lost and fell helplessly to the ground. Their groanings were so loud that Burke himself said he could not hear his own voice. The phenomena that characterized the Toronto Blessing, so far as I can tell, came apart from the preaching of eternal judgment. This does not invalidate the Toronto Blessing; it is a difference worth noting.

Second, the main result of people falling in Cane Ridge was their getting undoubted assurance of salvation. This came by the immediate and direct witness of the Holy Spirit. There was no intellectual process by which men and women needed to *conclude* they were saved; that is, no need to *reason*, e.g., "All who trust Christ's death on the cross are saved; I trust Christ's death, therefore I am saved." It was an immediate witness of the Spirit that bypassed reason that gave them this assurance. With the Toronto Blessing, however, assurance of salvation did not appear to have been a problem for most people to begin with, as far as I know, although this could have been the experience of some. The testimonies varied of those who were affected by the Toronto Blessing. Some laughed uncontrollably for several minutes, sometimes for an hour or more. It was a time of great joy and freedom. Assurance of salvation, then, was not an issue as far as I know; it was an experience that set people free from different kinds of bondage. Some professed physical healing. I know personally of a lot of people who received prophetic words while they were on the floor that changed their lives. I also know of some who did not particularly receive *any* conscious feeling; they simply fell because they "couldn't stand."

Third, whether in Logan County or Bourbon County, those falling exercises were always spontaneous. There was crying, laughing, shouting, jumping, running, and barking. The Toronto Blessing—which I supported and still do—was characterized by many of these manifestations except that they came largely, but not entirely, through the laying on of hands. Some criticize the Toronto Blessing because its manifestations mostly followed the laying on of hands. But people criticized the revivals in Logan and Bourbon Counties where the manifestations *were* spontaneous. There have always been the "antis" and there will always be. The lack of spontaneity does not nullify genuineness, but I think it is still a difference between Cane Ridge and Toronto that is worth noting. I would only add that the Toronto Blessing offers an invitation to become vulnerable—to see how earnest one is to get more of God. It can be humbling and embarrassing. Those who are adamantly against and opposed to this—as if waiting for God to knock them down spontaneously—will likely be passed by.

And if one is looking for a biblical basis for such unusual phenomena, consider these words, remembering too that God often offends the mind to reveal the heart:

> God chose the foolish things of the world to shame the wise; God chose the weak things of the world to shame the strong.
>
> —1 CORINTHIANS 1:27

> "For my thoughts are not your thoughts, neither are your ways my ways," declares the LORD. "As the heavens are higher than the earth, so are my ways higher than your ways and my thoughts than your thoughts."
>
> —ISAIAH 55:8–9

In this age of ever-increasing atheism, skepticism, unbelief, and absence of emphasis on God's wrath, the final judgment, and eternal punishment, I predict it will not be erudition or logic that will turn the tide. It won't be legislation by Parliament or Congress that will turn things around. Neither will it come by being seeker friendly or being overly cautious not to offend people. It will come through the unashamed proclamation of the God of the Bible and bold preaching of the pure gospel of Jesus Christ—*but* with power that is largely unseen today.

We truly need another Great Awakening. We must pray for power like what was observed in the day of John Wesley (1703–1791), Jonathan Edwards, and George Whitefield (1714–1770)—raw power similar to what I have written about in this chapter.

How far are we willing to go in our commitment to see the Holy Spirit come in power today? Or is the fear of man a greater influence on us?

How interested are we in being governed by an audience of One?

Are you willing to be the spark that could set a forest on fire?

Chapter Ten

WHEN YOU PERSONALLY SEE YOUR AUDIENCE OF ONE

❖

For I know that my Redeemer lives, and at the last he will
stand upon the earth. And after my skin has been thus
destroyed, yet in my flesh I shall see God, whom I shall see
for myself, and my eyes shall behold, and not another.
—Job 19:25–27, esv

WE BEGAN THIS book with the story of the child prodigal pianist who refused to bow to the applause of the standing audience because his teacher did not stand. He was playing for an audience of one—his teacher.

This book has been written with the hope that it will motivate you to wait for the praise that comes from the one and only true God—the "applause of the nail-scarred hands," as my friend put it. Not that one expects Jesus to clap for us, but I do know of one person He *stood* for—Stephen.

Stephen, one of the original seven deacons in the early church, was endued with an extraordinary anointing. When he was defending his theology before the Sanhedrin—the ruling council of the Jews—they could not resist "the wisdom the Spirit gave him" by which he spoke (Acts 6:10). His speaking was a perfect example of the Word and Spirit coming together simultaneously. That does not mean his hearers were converted. Far from it. As he was speaking, the Jews exploded. They were "furious and gnashed their teeth at him" (Acts 7:54). But, lo and behold, "full of the Holy Spirit," he "looked up to heaven and saw the glory of God, and Jesus standing at the right hand of God" (v. 55). Standing? Other references to Jesus at God's right hand show Him seated (Col. 3:1; Heb.1:3). I love Mrs. Martyn Lloyd-Jones's explanation: Jesus stood "to welcome the first martyr home." Moments later Stephen was stoned to death (Acts 7:60). What a way to go!

It is wonderful to remember that our Lord Jesus Christ at the right hand of God *notices* what is going on below! He is watching as He reigns. He is watching as He intercedes. He is watching when we suffer. He is watching when we laugh. He is watching as He waits, that is, as He waits for the day

He will return. When He comes back, coming in the clouds, "every eye will see him" (Rev. 1:7).

Get ready. You will see Him for yourself. Whatever will it be like? Will you be nervous? Will you be scared? Will you be thrilled? Will you be excited? Will you wish you had more time here on earth?

TWO CATEGORIES

How does one prepare for that day of days? First, there are two categories of people: saved and unsaved. The saved are those whose sins have been washed away by the blood of Jesus Christ. They are those who transferred their trust in good works to what Jesus did for them on the cross, namely, His paying our debt to God.

Are you saved? Do you know for sure that if you were to die today that you would go to heaven? If God were to ask you, "Why should I let you into My heaven?" what would you say? If your true and honest answer would *not* be that you are trusting in the death of Jesus on the cross, please pray this (if you truly mean these words in your heart of hearts):

> *Lord Jesus Christ, I need You. I want You. I know*
> *I am a sinner. I am sorry for my sins. Thank You*
> *for dying for me on the cross. Wash my sins away by*
> *Your blood. I welcome Your Holy Spirit into my heart.*
> *As best as I know how, I give You my life. Amen.*

It is my prayer that all who read these lines and pray this prayer will be led by the Holy Spirit from this day to:

1. Read your Bible every day.

2. Pray daily to God the Father in the name of Jesus.

3. Witness for Christ daily; let people know you are unashamed of Him.

4. Remember that your relationship with other people has changed because you are a new creation.

5. Find a church or fellowship of Christians where the Bible is revered as the Word of God.

The unsaved, sadly, will go into eternal punishment for their sins. There are basically two ways God punishes sin: either by the blood of His Son the Lord Jesus Christ or by eternal damnation in hell. That is what the Bible teaches. Hell was prepared for the devil and his angels (Matt. 25:41), but those who have not received Jesus Christ will spend eternity with them; they "will go away to eternal punishment, but the righteous to eternal life" (v. 46).

But how do the *saved* prepare to meet this One "whom having not seen you love" (1 Pet. 1:8, NKJV)? It will be without doubt the scariest day of our lives. And yet John poses the possibility of having "confidence on the day of judgment" (1 John 4:17). Obviously Stephen, just before he died, was affirmed by Jesus Himself. Countless saints over the centuries have testified to having great assurance as they died. John Wesley had an answer for his critics: "Our people die well."[1]

The two categories, then, are saved and unsaved. All will die. The greatest and most important question anybody can put to you is this: Where will you be one hundred years from now? We are all going to die.

This will happen when your time is up. It is a grim but also glorious reminder that we won't be on this planet forever. You and I have in common that it will be decided in heaven when our time is up. We may feel we have not had enough time. I will never forget a word from Dr. Clyde Francisco (1916–1981), my Old Testament professor at Southern Baptist Theological Seminary, a man who loved God and whom I admired greatly. He once said to his class, "We all feel that we don't have enough time. The truth is God gives all of us enough time."

I believe that. However long we live, God will have given us enough time.

When the apostle Peter was apprehended by King Herod, he was imprisoned and chained. Not only that, but four squads guarded him. He fell asleep in prison between two soldiers; he was bound with two chains. Prayer went up for him by the church. Suddenly he was miraculously delivered. An angel of the Lord stood next to him and a light shone in the cell. "Get up quickly," the angel said. "Wrap your cloak around you and follow me" (Acts 12:7–8, esv). They passed through the first and second guard. When they came to the iron gate, it "opened for them by itself" (v. 10). In a word, Peter was delivered and showed himself to those who were praying for him (vv. 12–17). But a day would come when no angel would do this for Peter. Jesus foretold Peter's death: "When you are old you will stretch out your hands, and someone else will dress you and lead you where you do not want to go" (John 21:18).

In other words, there would come a day when Peter's time would be up. Even for Peter, when God was finished with him, the same God who had miraculously delivered him earlier would now let him die. Peter was crucified in Rome. The report of his death states that he asked to be crucified upside down as he felt he was not worthy to be crucified like his Lord.

God gives all of us enough time. And when our time is up, there is not a thing we can do to stop it.

The one phrase in the Bible *all* of humankind will agree with is this: "It is appointed unto men once to die" (Heb. 9:27, KJV). We are all going to die. But the second part of that verse is what is equally true—like it or not: "after this the judgment" (KJV).

TWO SHOWINGS

It is the final judgment to which the writer refers in Hebrews 9:27. Also called "the judgment seat of Christ" (2 Cor. 5:10), you and I will be there to stand before the Lord Jesus Christ. He came the first time to die on a cross for our sins; He will come "a second time, not to bear sin, but to bring salvation to those who are waiting for him" (Heb. 9:28).

But there is more; not all are eagerly waiting for Him. I now return to the subject of the unsaved. There are those who don't believe in Him. There are those who deny Him. There are those who rejected Him. They too will see Him. Even though they did not govern their lives to honor the audience of One, they will literally see Him:

> Behold, he is coming with the clouds, and every eye will see him, even those who pierced him, and all tribes of the earth will wail on account of him.
>
> —REVELATION 1:7, ESV

181

This will be a public showing of Jesus. Revelation 1:7 refers to the second coming and that general reaction of people who witness this. "Every eye" will see Him—the living, the dead, the rich, the poor, the saved, the lost, the white, the black, kings, common people; every person who ever lived will witness this. How? They will have been raised from the dead when Jesus leaves His position at God's right hand and shows Himself with the clouds as promised. Even those who pierced Him. This refers to those who nailed Him to the cross—both Jews and Gentiles. It is a way of showing that *no one* will escape the judgment seat of Christ.

The reason that people will "wail" is because they will see that Jesus Christ truly lived and died and has now come to show Himself to the world. It will be a vindication of Jesus Christ—an open vindication of who Jesus is. It will be a vindication of the Bible. It will cause all people to see how they loved darkness rather than light because their deeds were evil. They will know they are going to be eternally condemned. They will wail—the sound of extreme distraught and regret and hopelessness will be heard by all. There will be no attempt to hide one's grief; there will be no effort to protect one's sophistication or dignity. They will scream; they will cry out; they will plead for mercy. But it will be too late. That is why they will wail on that day of days.

Moreover, this is what John the Baptist meant by his message: "Who warned you to flee from the coming wrath?" (Matt. 3:7). Had you realized that the first message in the New Testament refers to the wrath of God? Furthermore Paul gives the primary reason people should be Christians: *because of the wrath of God*. Having stated that he is not ashamed of the gospel (Rom. 1:16) and then giving an outline of the gospel in

Romans 1:17, Paul states: "For [Greek *gar*, meaning because] the wrath of God is revealed" (v. 18, ESV). Indeed, Paul went on to state that we are justified by Christ's blood—we are "saved from God's wrath through him" (Rom. 5:9). Salvation is about being saved from the "coming wrath" (1 Thess. 1:10). Jesus asked those who rejected Him, "How will you escape being condemned to hell?" (Matt. 23:33).

Is it not sad that this clear, plain message of the New Testament seems to have been swept under the carpet by the church today? I honestly fear and truly believe our day is a fulfillment of Paul's words: "The time will come when people will not put up with sound doctrine. Instead, to suit their own desires, they will gather around them a great number of teachers to say what their itching ears want to hear" (2 Tim. 4:3).

In any case the message of John the Baptist, Jesus, and Paul will be clearly unveiled when Jesus personally comes again.

That is what I mean by the public showing of Jesus.

However, there will be another showing of Jesus—for the saved. There will be two categories of saved people: those who will receive a reward and those who will not receive a reward at the judgment seat of Christ. Those who will not receive a reward will "suffer loss" of such a reward but be saved by fire (1 Cor. 3:15). This means they will go to heaven and not go to hell. The fire will burn up the works that were done in the flesh. Paul said, "Their work will be shown for what it is, because the Day will bring it to light. It will be revealed with fire, and the fire will test the quality of each person's work" (1 Cor. 3:13).

Some say, "I don't care whether I receive a reward at the judgment seat of Christ. I just want to go to heaven when I die." I do understand that. Caution: you won't feel that way then! Standing before the Lord Jesus Christ with no reward will find us grieving with incalculable sorrow on that day. No reward is the consequence of choices we made on earth: receiving "what is due us for the things done while in the body, whether good or bad" (2 Cor. 5:10). Absence of reward will be evident because we lived selfishly, carelessly, and desiring the praise and approval of people rather than seeking the praise that comes from the only God. In a word, loss of reward can be traced to showing indifference to living for an audience of One.

The reward (also called prize, inheritance, or crown—1 Cor. 9:24; Col. 3:24; 2 Tim. 4:8) was very important to Paul, so much so that he said, "I strike a blow to my body and make it my slave so that after I have preached to others, I myself will not be disqualified for the prize" (1 Cor. 9:27). If Paul regarded a reward as important, so should you and I. Not only that, but it will not honor our Lord if we face Him having not chosen to live for an audience of One.

Those who will receive a reward will be those who lived for an audience of One.

What will the person of Jesus be like when He comes a second time "not to bear sin" (Heb. 9:28)? It will be the same Jesus (Acts 1:11). He Himself said, "Look, I am coming soon! My reward is with me, and I will give to each person according to what they have done" (Rev. 22:12). John on the Isle of Patmos had a vision of Jesus that indicates what Jesus will be like when He comes the second time: "His eyes were like blazing fire" (Rev. 1:14). That shows how Jesus feels about sin. It also shows how and why He viewed the seven churches as He did in Revelation 2 and 3. It gives a picture of Jesus that mirrors both the compassion and wrath the God the Father.

That is the One before whom you and I will stand.

Think about it. You and I who are saved *will* stand before Jesus Christ Himself. We will stand before the very One we will have either affirmed as being our audience of One or did not take very seriously. What a supreme privilege!

PREPARING FOR THE JUDGMENT SEAT

At the beginning of this book I promised to show the way forward—how we may avoid the deep regret that is possible at the judgment seat of Christ.

I will summarize what I have taught in this book like this:

1. Be *grateful*. God loves gratitude. Paul reminded us that when we pray, we should put our prayer and petition before Him "with thanksgiving" (Phil. 4:6). God loves gratitude. He notices ingratitude. Never forget that when Jesus healed ten lepers and only one came back to thank Him, Jesus immediately said, "Were not all ten cleansed? Where are the other nine?" (Luke 17:17). That is a sobering reminder that God notices when we forget to thank Him.

2. Be *generous*. Be a good giver—first to His church but also to all who uphold the gospel and who need our support. Furthermore remember the poor. It is a truism and a biblical promise: "Whoever sows sparingly will also reap sparingly, and whoever sows generously will also reap generously.... God loves a cheerful [Greek *hilaros*] giver" (2 Cor. 9:6–7). Remember too that Abraham was the

first tither; the gospel puts all of us back to
Abraham's position. He gave out of gratitude,
not because he was trying to endear himself. Those who choose to live on 90 percent
of their income not only honor God but are
blessed immeasurably.

3. Be *gracious*. That means to let people off the
hook when they may well deserve to have the
book thrown at them. It is total forgiveness,
setting those people free who wanted to harm
you. It is praying for them—that they will be
blessed. The dividends from living like this
are incalculable. Here are three rules you may
follow: first, it is never wrong to be gracious;
second, it is never wrong to be gracious; third,
it is never wrong to be gracious.

When you struggle to live by these principles, simply remember
you are doing all these things for an audience of One.

FOR PREACHERS ONLY

It is impossible to know how many ministers and preachers of
the gospel will read this book. But may I say a word to ministers? It was the audience of One that Paul had in mind when
he preached:

> Unlike so many, we do not peddle the word of God for
> profit....In Christ we speak before God with sincerity,
> as those sent from God.
>
> —2 CORINTHIANS 2:17

The verse reads, "We speak before God." All ministers know what it is like to have a prestigious person in the audience when they preach. It is hard not to think of that person. You try not to look at the person. You wonder if he or she will like what you say. You may look out of the corner of your eye when you make a particular point to see if the person seems to nod with approval or stares straight ahead.

Or consider this: if you spoke at St. George's Chapel at Windsor Castle with Her Majesty, the Queen, present, who could help but be conscious of her presence? In your preparation you would consider every sentence carefully. When you speak, you would want to be sure your tone of voice, mannerisms, and volume are entirely suitable before royalty. (In case you are wondering, that has not happened to me, but I am imagining what it might be like.)

Paul says that when he preaches, he speaks *before God*, that is, as to an audience of One. It is the Lord God whom he wants to be conscious of when he speaks.

I so want to be like that. Any preacher worth his salt would want to be like that—to speak to an audience of One no matter who is present or how many people are present.

One further word to ministers, vicars, pastors, and evangelists: How much do you pray? Remember how Jesus affirmed Mary for wanting to sit at Jesus' feet. Martha complained that she was having to do all the work while Mary just wanted to be with Jesus. He said, "Martha, Martha...you are worried and upset about many things, but few things are needed—or indeed only one. Mary has chosen what is better, and it will not be taken away from her" (Luke 10:41–42).

My advice to those in the ministry: be like Mary. Martin Luther prayed two hours a day, sometimes more. John Wesley prayed at least two hours a day. But where are the Luthers today? Where are the Wesleys?

Children spell *love* T-I-M-E. How much time do you have for God? There will be no praying in heaven. Worship? Yes. Prayer? No.

I now come to the end of my book. It is my prayer that I have written in a manner that will make a difference for good in your life.

CONCLUSION

I T HAS NOT easy been easy to do—to write a book for a readership of One while knowing people like you would read this. To put it another way, I have imagined Him looking over my shoulder as I wrote. This has caused me to leave a lot out I might have written but also to say things I had not intended to say. Do not take this to mean that I think God has written this book or that I have heard Him perfectly! As Brother Lawrence can speak of the practice of the presence of God, so I have sought to practice hearing God as I wrote. Only a fool would claim to be writing a postcanonical book under divine inspiration. It would be the equivalent of a person saying, "The Lord told me," when uttering a word to someone.

One of my publishers told me one of his writers objected to being edited since all that was written was what God wrote! Believe me, I welcome critical feedback and all the editing that my publisher deems appropriate. Whether this quest has made what you have read a better book than all my others, I have no idea. And whether this venture has pleased Him more, I tremble to contemplate. The heart is so deceitful and desperately wicked; who can know it? (Jer. 17:9).

In any case that's it for now.

> *May the grace of our Lord Jesus Christ, the love and tender mercy of God the Father, and the blessing of the Holy Spirit who applies the sprinkling of Christ's blood on you be yours now and evermore. Amen.*

NOTES

SPECIAL RECOMMENDATION

1. "*The World Is Not Enough* Quotes," Rotten Tomatoes, accessed October 21, 2019, https://www.rottentomatoes.com/m/world_is_not_enough/quotes/.

CHAPTER ONE
WHAT'S IN IT FOR GOD?

1. Fanny Crosby, "Pass Me Not, O Gentle Savior."
2. Jonathan Edwards, *The Works of Jonathan Edwards* vol. 2 (Edinburgh, UK: Banner of Truth Trust, 1974), https://ccel.org/ccel/edwards/works2/works2.vi.i.html.

CHAPTER TWO
KNOWING THAT GOD KNOWS

1. Martyn Lloyd-Jones, *Romans: An Exposition of Chapter 14:1–17 Liberty and Conscience* (Carlisle, PA: Banner of Truth Trust, 2007), xi.
2. Anna Letitia Waring, "In Heavenly Love Abiding."
3. Joseph M. Scriven, "What a Friend We Have in Jesus."
4. William Shakespeare, *Hamlet*, 3.2.254.

Chapter Three
Vindication

1. *Oxford Dictionary of Modern Quotations* (Oxford, UK: Oxford University Press, 2007), 313.
2. Robert Robinson, "Come, Thou Fount of Every Blessing."
3. Frances R. Havergal, "Like a River Glorious."

Chapter Four
The Greatest Goal on Earth

1. Horatius Bonar, "Go, Labor On."

Chapter Five
Integrity

1. Charles Moore, "Who, in This Swollen and Ever-Widening Field, Can Truly Claim To Be a Tory?," *Daily Telegraph*, June 3, 2019, https://www.telegraph.co.uk/politics/2019/06/03/swollen-ever-widening-field-can-truly-claim-tory/.
2. Moore, "Who, in This Swollen and Ever-Widening Field, Can Truly Claim To Be a Tory?"
3. Margaret Jenkins Harris, "I Will Praise Him."
4. Charles Krauthammer, *The Point of It All*, ed. Daniel Krauthammer (New York: Crown Forum, 2018), xxx.
5. Sam Hailes, "Jackie Pullinger: 'We're Going to Feel Stupid for Eternity if We Waste This Life,'" *Premier Christianity*, January 19, 2019, https://www.premierchristianity.com/Past-Issues/2019/January-2019/Jackie-Pullinger-We-re-going-to-feel-stupid-for-eternity-if-we-waste-this-life.
6. "A Brief History of WEC International," WEC International, accessed October 20, 2019, https://www.wec-usa.org/history/.

7. Blue Letter Bible, s.v. *"stigma,"* accessed October 24, 2019, https://www.blueletterbible.org/lang/lexicon/lexicon.cfm?t=kjv&strongs=g4742.

8. Billy Graham, "What's 'the Billy Graham Rule'?," BGEA, July 23, 2019, https://billygraham.org/story/the-modesto-manifesto-a-declaration-of-biblical-integrity/.

9. "Interview With Pastor Rick Warren and Pastor John Piper," Saddleback Valley Community Church, May 1, 2011, http://pastors.com/wp-content/uploads/2011/12/JohnPiperInterviewPastorRickWarrenTranscript.pdf.

CHAPTER SIX
THE INTEGRITY OF JESUS

1. "Apostles' Creed: Traditional and Ecumenical Versions," United Methodist Church, accessed October 21, 2019, http://www.umc.org/what-we-believe/apostles-creed-traditional-ecumenical.

2. Isaac Watts, "Alas! and Did My Savior Bleed."

3. Charles Wesley, "And Can It Be."

4. "Didache," Early Christian Writings, accessed October 21, 2019, http://www.earlychristianwritings.com/text/didache-roberts.html.

CHAPTER SEVEN
CHARACTER AND GIFTING

1. John Calvin, *Institutes of the Christian Religion*, ed. John T. McNeill (Louisville, KY: Westminster John Knox Press, 2006), https://books.google.com/books?id=0aB1BwAAQBAJ&pg.

Chapter Eight
The Faith Hall of Fame

1. Blue Letter Bible, s.v. *"hypostasis,"* accessed October 21, 2019, https://www.blueletterbible.org/lang/lexicon/lexicon.cfm?Strongs=G5287&t=NIV
2. *Apologeticum*, The Tertullian Project, accessed October 22, 2019, http://www.tertullian.org/works/apologeticum.htm.

Chapter Nine
A Spark

1. James Smith, *History of the Christian Church, From Its Origin to the Present Time; Compiled From Various Authors* (Nashville: Cumberland Presbyterian Office, 1835), 672–673, https://archive.org/details/historyofchristifit00smit/page/672.
2. Scott Harp, "The Work and Influence of Barton Warren Stone," History of the Restoration Movement, accessed October 24, 2019, https://www.therestorationmovement.com/lessons/chlesson06.htm.
3. Smith, *History of the Christian Church*, 565–566.
4. James McGready, "Narrative of the Commencement and Progress of the Revival of 1800," October 23, 1801, http://www.cumberland.org/hfcpc/McGreaBK.htm#anchor222019.
5. McGready, "Narrative of the Commencement and Progress of the Revival of 1800."
6. W. F. P. Noble, *A Century of Gospel-Work: A History of the Growth of Evangelical Religion in the United States* (Philadelphia: H. C. Watts, 1876), 232, https://books.google.com/books?id=oWw_AQAAMAAJ&pg.
7. Smith, *History of the Christian Church*, 571.
8. Noble, *A Century of Gospel-Work*, 232.
9. John McGee, "Commencement of the Great Revival of Religion in Kentucky and Tennessee, in 1799, in a

Letter to the Rev. Thomas L. Douglass," June 23, 1820, in *The Methodist Magazine*, vol. 4 (New York: N. Bangs and T. Mason, 1821), 190, https://books.google.com/books?id=zekWAQAAIAAJ&pg.

10. McGee, "Commencement of the Great Revival of Religion in Kentucky and Tennessee."

11. McGee, "Commencement of the Great Revival of Religion in Kentucky and Tennessee."

12. Noble, *A Century of Gospel-Work*, 232.

13. McGee, "Commencement of the Great Revival of Religion in Kentucky and Tennessee."

14. McGee, "Commencement of the Great Revival of Religion in Kentucky and Tennessee."

15. Frank Masters, "The Great Revival of 1800 in Kentucky," Baptist History Homepage, 1953, http://baptisthistoryhomepage.com/ky.baptists.masters.chp9.revival.html.

16. James Ross, *Life and Times of Elder Reuben Ross* (Philadelphia: Grant, Faires & Rodgers, 1882), 234, https://books.google.com/books?id=u5k-AAAAYAAJ&dq.

17. Ross, *Life and Times of Elder Reuben Ross*, 234.

18. Barton Warren Stone, *The Biography of Eld. Barton Warren Stone* (Cincinnati: J. A. & U. P. James, 1847), 39.

19. Sarah Pierrepont Edwards, "Her Uncommon Discoveries of the Divine Perfections and Glory; and of the Excellency of Christ," from Sereno Dwight, *The Works of President Edwards: With a Memoir of His Life*, vol. 1 (New York: G. & C. & H. Carvill, 1830), 171–190, https://digital.library.upenn.edu/women/pierrepont/conversion/conversion.html.

20. Stone, *The Biography of Eld. Barton Warren Stone*, 37.

21. As quoted in Masters, "The Great Revival of 1800 in Kentucky."

22. Stone, *The Biography of Eld. Barton Warren Stone*, 34–35.

23. Albert Henry Redford, *The History of Methodism in Kentucky* (Nashville: Southern Methodist Publishing House, 1870), 357, https://books.google.com/books?id=YJHba-YRhtIC&pg.

24. Redford, *The History of Methodism in Kentucky*, 357
    –358.
25. James Bradley Finley, *The Autobiography of Rev. James B.
    Finley* (Bedford, MA: Applewood Books, 2009), 166.
26. Stone, *The Biography of Eld. Barton Warren Stone*, 38.

CHAPTER TEN
WHEN YOU PERSONALLY SEE YOUR AUDIENCE OF ONE

1. Kenneth W. Osbeck, *101 More Hymn Stories* (Grand
   Rapids, MI: Kregel, 1985), 14.